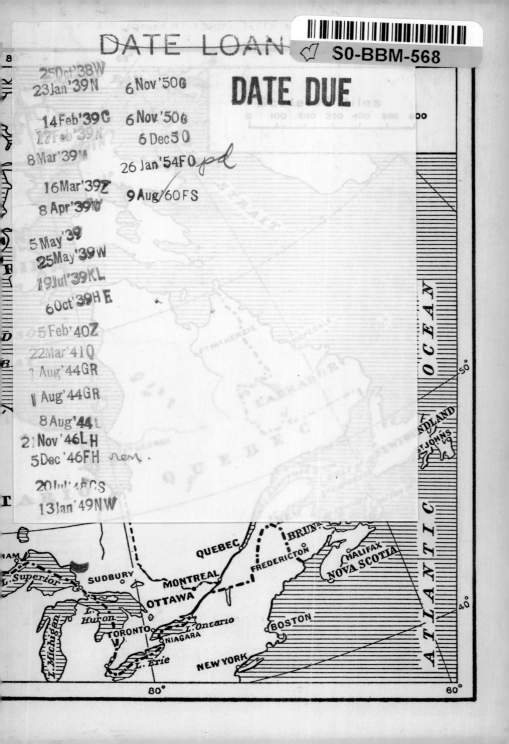

CANADA

CANADA
by André Siegfried

TRANSLATED FROM THE FRENCH BY

H. H. Hemming & Doris Hemming

HARCOURT, BRACE AND COMPANY

NEW YORK

Designed by Robert Josephy

PRINTED IN THE UNITED STATES OF AMERICA

BY QUINN & BODEN COMPANY, INC., RAHWAY, N. J.

CONTENTS

5

IV

THE POLITICAL ASPECT

MAPS

PREFACE

EXACTLY thirty years have passed since I published a book entitled *Le Canada, les Deux Races*. Before embarking upon this study of contemporary political problems, I had concluded my third trip to Canada. My first was made as early as 1898.

I do not propose to bring this earlier book up to date, for so much water has flowed under the bridges since then that mere revision would not suffice. Nor do I intend to write a book on the same lines as before, because the psychological analysis which I then made of the two groups, English and French, still holds good today. When one penetrates deep enough, one finds that peoples change very little. I should simply be repeating myself, and that is the negation of intellectual work.

I believe, however, that there remains another book to be written—a book about a new Canada which scarcely existed at the beginning of the century. The British Commonwealth, which formerly consisted of a sovereign metropolis and its colonies, has now become a federation of autonomous nations, equal in rank, and virtually independent. On Vimy and other battlefields of the Great War Canada acquired, one might even say conquered, an international status which was confirmed by her admittance as a distinct political entity into the League of Nations.

In the present book then, I propose to limit myself to this new aspect of Canada which is international, not merely American or British as in the past. I shall not undertake either a geographical or historical study of Canada, nor shall I make an economic inventory, nor even a political analysis. My subject is at once wider and more restricted in scope, for I shall try to describe the international position of Canada in the economic and political equilibrium of the twentieth century. I shall study her geographical contacts, her racial structure, her place in world markets as both producer and consumer, the possibilities awaiting her in the realm of culture, her exceptional role of interpreter between the United States and England, and finally, her chance of survival as an independent nation.

Since the publication of my first book I have made several more journeys to Canada, and I have followed its evolution with the same intense interest that I previously devoted to studying the regime of Sir Wilfrid Laurier, which now seems so long ago. I spent the year 1915 with the First Canadian Heavy Battery, acting as interpreter for the Canadian Army in France. Shortly after the Armistice I was a member of a Mission which was sent by the French Government to the Canadian

Government. I have now crossed Canada from Quebec to Victoria three times, in 1914, in 1919, and in 1935. I have seen the Canadian people in prosperity and in depression, in war and in peace, at home and abroad.

The singular complexity of a country which is American geographically, British politically, largely French in origin, and yet world-wide in its international preoccupations, seems to afford the subject matter for an absorbing study. Although the present book is entirely different from my earlier one, it may also be considered its sequel.

I

THE GEOGRAPHICAL
ASPECT

CHAPTER I

EUROPE AND AMERICA
CONTRASTED

§ 1

AT the beginning, in the middle, and at the end of any study of Canada, one must reiterate that Canada is American. History occasionally loses sight of this fact, but at every step geography imperiously recalls it. And yet a political bond does exist with the Old World, and herein lies the novelty and originality of the Canadian problem.

Everyone knows that the continents of Europe and America do not resemble one another; in fact the very atmosphere is different. To appreciate America a European observer must change his mental attitude, his sense of proportion, and even his vocabulary. Our idioms no longer apply, in fact we almost hesitate to use them in these new surroundings. European civilization rests on a triple foundation of race, culture, and methods of production. Our culture comes from the Greeks whose intellectual tradition we have inherited. Our ideal of the individual is derived immediately from the eighteenth century, but fundamentally it arises out of Christianity itself, which taught us the now somewhat jeopardized doctrine of respect for the human being. Our industrial methods, even allowing for recent Americanizations, have also emerged from eighteenth-century craftsmanship, which saw the birth of the steam engine, of the division of labour, and of mass production. The spirit of invention, the refusal to submit to the inevitable, individualism concealing the germ of revolt which in itself is creative—all these things are characteristic of the European genius.

One may say that such characteristics are equally applicable to the whole of western civilization—to the whole of the white race, overflowing, as it now does, the borders of Europe. True, but this magnificent civilization, which has transformed the world in the past, could have arisen, and can continue to thrive, only under certain clearly-defined geographical conditions. There is also no doubt that it could have evolved only by the incomparable artisanship of the white race. Further than that, however, it required the framework of a continent constructed, as it were, in human proportions, being big without being colossal, and where Nature itself is never overpowering, never out of proportion to man himself.

"The statement of Protagoras, that *man is the measure of things*," writes M. Paul Valéry, "is characteristic, and essentially Mediterranean."

Could we also say "European"? In our old continent we have the impression that Man dominates Nature, and that he has tamed and civilized her to a point where she no longer appears under her original guise. But, in conquering Nature the European has adapted himself to her. He understands and respects the inexorable laws of Time, which have taught him to build solidly. The past is always present in this part of the world, even when we turn towards the future, for our culture is based on tradition. We navigate in deep waters like a boat with three thousand years under her keel. It is this maturity, which we share with Asia, that distinguishes us from America. The price we pay for it is an economic depletion, a gradual impoverishment of the possibilities of Nature, and a reduction of the margin between the actual and the potential.

Out of this arise unmistakable consequences, both social and political. As the burden of producing wealth becomes steadily heavier one naturally wonders if it would not be easier to share existing wealth rather than create anew: the slightest additional effort makes for revolution. Also, in our over-crowded continent, quarrels over territory take on a bitterness which the peoples of sparsely populated countries do not understand. With us a war of conquest is an ever-present menace.

When we turn to America what strikes us, in contrast, is the grandeur, the vastness of Nature. The new continent is not built on the same scale as ours. Niagara, the St. Lawrence, the Grand Canyon of the Colorado, the western prairies, are more like Asia or Africa than like our countryside. To find anything approaching the same scenery in Europe, we must go far to the north or to the east—into Scandinavia where there are pre-Cambrian massifs resembling the Canadian Laurentian Shield, or into the immensity of Russia, which really is not European at all.

Europe is delicately moulded, like a hand with tapering fingers outstretched towards the sea; America has the contour of a massive fist, or a heavy piece of furniture, solid but unadorned. In the New World Nature dwarfs Man. He is not fashioned on that same vast scale, though he is apt to boast too soon that he has been able to overcome the elements.

The relationship between the American and the forces of Nature with which he must contend has profoundly marked his attitude, his reactions, and his psychology. The man of the New World is nearer to primitive Nature than we are. Though he may be better equipped as regards the comforts of life, yet at heart he is simpler. His apparent conquest of Nature, brilliant and rapid though it may be, is deceptive. In his haste he refuses to recognize obstacles. He brutally attacks Nature and, in so doing, fails to appreciate her. Are we quite sure that he has subdued her? We realize, though he himself may not, that the lack of a peasant civilization indicates the American farmer's inability to identify himself with the soil he tills. The American is impatient of delay. He does not believe the proverb that warns: Time always has its revenge. So both the rhythm and the social atmosphere of Europe and America are completely different because the two continents are not of the same age.

Everyone knows—or believes, for it may not be true —that individual success is possible in the existing order, and since it is easier to produce than to distribute, the law of least resistance makes Americans conservative. Why fight to obtain territory when there is already more than can be developed? Being already so richly endowed, the Americans are not interested in conquest. To them European wars and the fortification of frontiers, seems incredible, useless, and fundamentally wrong. "How wicked these Europeans are!" they say to themselves. Obviously it is not only two continents, but two different ages that are at variance. We are mature, almost old; the Americans are young, so young that they sometimes seem puerile. Each of the two worlds approaches problems from an entirely different angle. Are we really contemporaries?

I have spoken of the white race, of Europe, of the West; but the meaning of these terms varies, and must be defined. At one time they were synonymous: when the white race was limited to Europe, and when Europe consisted of the entire Western World. Since the sixteenth, and especially since the eighteenth century, this co-relation has been disappearing. Examined closely, not all of Europe appears western in the sense in which we have tried to define Western traditions. East of Vienna and the Elbe—or east of the Oder if you prefer —where we first come into contact with Nature on a grandiose scale asserting her rights against Man, we have the impression that we are no longer in Europe. Here the influence of Greece and Rome, in the shadow of which Christianity was developed, is no longer uncontested. The regions which were dominated by Rome are easily distinguishable, for the others are of a different hue. We may wish to believe in the unity of Europe, but even if we do succeed in maintaining it or re-establishing it, it will no longer coincide with the unity of western civilization as a whole.

The white race is no longer entirely European, since one branch has developed and prospered overseas. Now that it has spread beyond Europe's confines and adapted itself to new geographic conditions which are bound in the long run to transform it, our western civilization may continue to be racial, but it is no longer continental. Out of this fact has arisen the conception of a Western World extending beyond our continental boundaries—one in which the centre of gravity cannot be exactly defined. The British Empire is a symptom of this shifting, since it is no longer strictly English.

These somewhat subtle distinctions serve to modify the fine unity of the simple terms, Europe and America. Yet they allow us to maintain a bridge between the two continents, and, in so doing, lead us to a better understanding of such European characteristics as have a chance of survival in the New World.

§ 2

We have discussed the contrast between Europe and America; let us now examine another fundamental topic, namely, the unity of the entire American continent, North and South. In common parlance one speaks of "the Americas" as if the two were quite distinct. But I personally have always felt that their difference is less marked than their resemblance, and that there is an atmosphere common to all the countries of the New World, due mainly to the very fact that they are new.

Show me in the United States, in Canada, or in the Argentine, even one landscape which resembles Western or Central Europe or the Mediterranean! To a geographer who already knows the North, South America does not appear strange. The Andes and the Rockies are the same mountain range. If we could fold one continent over on top of the other, we should find an amazing similarity. Chile would correspond to British Columbia, both having forests, fiords, and glaciers; Peru would find its counterpart in California with tawny barren hills intersected by oases; and finally the high Andean plateaux in Peru, Colombia, and Venezuela are remarkably like Utah, Arizona and Mexico.

On the Atlantic side we find the same symmetry, though less accentuated. The tropical atmosphere, humid and sombre, of Brazil, occurs again not only in the Antilles but also in Louisiana, and even reaches Alabama and Georgia. In a sense, the distinction between the Pacific and the Atlantic coast is more marked than the difference between the two hemispheres. In the great plains the same striking resemblance between north and south appears at every turn. The Argentine pampas are like the American and Canadian prairies, having the same vast open spaces, the same clear sky, and the same crops; one seems to be back in the Dakotas, or Saskatchewan. And similarly, as one approaches the mountains near Mendoza or Cordoba, one inevitably thinks of Denver or Calgary.

Thus the geographic relationship of the two continents is obvious. The Latin and Anglo-Saxon peoples in the New World both tread the same soil, breathe the same air, produce and market the same goods in the same economic conditions, and react to international problems in the same way. Pan-Americanism, in so far as it is free from the taint of imperialism, expresses the fundamentals of this continental sistership. Canada belongs to this great family, notwithstanding the fact that she is distinguished from the other American countries by a geographical peculiarity. It so happens that, as both continents are wide in the north and taper off in the south, the northern hemisphere has more arctic regions and the southern hemisphere has more tropics. Owing to the immense northland, to which there is no counterpart in the southern hemisphere, Canada is unique among the nations of the New World, and is therefore somewhat tempted to stand apart from the others.

The resemblance between the two Americas that I have stressed so far is geographical. Historically they have followed separate paths. The Anglo-Saxon Protestants of the North, and the Latin Catholics of the South, have produced distinct civilizations, each retaining in one way and another the marks of their origin. As a result there are at work in the Americas two distinct influences, which are contradictory rather than complementary. The first, historical, produces the same type of civilization in America as in Europe, and the other, geographical, tends on the contrary to separate the continents by giving America a personality that is becoming increasingly distinct from Europe. The Americas seem to have a north-south axis, and also an east-west one. The former is geographic and is the principal one because it results from the very conformation of the continents themselves. It is expressed by the majestic geological folds, by the vertical arrangement of the climatic zones, and by the natural trend of commerce. It is even to be seen in the flow of public opinion. One feels that its effects are inevitable, and that, in the end, it will overcome all resistance.

Such are the views of the eminent geographer, M. Baulig, who declares that while a relief map of Europe shows that traffic of every kind moves east and west along the parallels of latitude, in North America circulation develops more readily north and south along the meridians of longitude. Climatic conditions vary gradually and imperceptibly as we pass from north to south, but they are precise and distinct when we go across the continent from east to west, and particularly when we come to the western mountain ranges. Although the white races continued their trans-Atlantic migrations by marching steadily westward along the parallels of latitude, and although this historical fact has been perpetuated by political frontiers and the railway lines, yet, on the other hand, contrary currents also exist, currents which are more in conformity with the physical nature of the continent in its fundamental division into east, centre, and west. This division arises from the architectural structure of the continent, and it cannot be obliterated by technical manipulation.[1]

If, according to M. Baulig's vigorous thesis, the north-south axis is inherent in the architectural structure of the continent, the east-west axis, on the contrary, is essentially historical and artificial; it is maintained more by momentum than by the nature of things. It is thus that the initial influence of Europe with its own geographic division into Mediterranean and Nordic, has been perpetuated in these new territories, though in point of fact this European influence is becoming more and more foreign as the years go by.

Which axis will prevail in the end? Will geography finally efface the play of history? If so, the American nations will gradually become more alike, Pan-Americanism will prevail, and possibly there will be no Canada. If history, on the contrary, succeeds in maintaining its hold indefinitely, Europe will remain a factor in the destinies of America. By overcoming a gravitation which now seems irresistible, Canada will fall back on her east-west axis, and will maintain a separate existence and a personality of her own.

It is under the symbol of the compass, therefore, that we must embark on any serious study of America, and consequently of Canada.

We are fully aware of the difficulties of the task.

[1] *Geographie Universelle*, Vol. XIII (North America, p. 5).

In order to speak with any assurance of the continent of America, one must appreciate its sense of proportion, which is different from ours; its climate, which seems frankly exotic to us; its colours and its perfumes; its rhythm, and above all its *tempo,* which is a combination of feverishness, optimism, and lightheartedness, and which is not attuned to our more fragile equilibrium.

And yet we must not turn our backs entirely on old Europe. Aside from the factors of geography, if we wish to comprehend America fully, we must hark back to its spiritual sources, which had their origin in the Old World. In order to understand Canada profoundly, we must examine English puritanism, the Anglican church, and the French Catholic tradition. It is a delicate task to decide what must be attributed to geography, and what to tradition. In this continent of quantities any admixture of qualities must be subtle. It reminds one of certain complex atmospheres in the Near East.

The Canadian problem—for there is one—arises from this duality, which is more marked there than anywhere else in the New World. Canada, as we were at pains to recall in the opening sentence of this study, is American; and yet it is the only country in America which has kept a non-American political allegiance. A unique relationship with both the United States and the British Empire has resulted from this diversity of ties. Canada has maintained excellent contacts, and as a result, in spite of her small population, she has a political influence which we must be careful not to under-estimate.

CHAPTER II

GEOGRAPHY AND THE
CANADIAN PROBLEM

THAT there should be a country called Canada, distinct from the United States, is a mere accident of history, in fact, a political paradox. Nature has not conferred upon Canada any particular personality of its own. There is no geographical difference to separate it from its great neighbour to the south. It is a problem to determine wherein lies Canada's centre of gravity: politically it is in England, and geographically it is in the United States—in either case outside its own boundaries. Its very existence is connected with this problem; for a purely British Canada could never be anything but a colony, and an American Canada could only be a group of states in the Union. Later we shall discuss the political relationship with England, but first let us fix Canada's position geographically in the American continent, a continent, which, as we have already pointed out, possesses remarkable unity.

§ 1

From a geographical point of view Canada is merely the northern extension of the United States. There is no natural boundary between the two countries, but merely a political frontier along the parallel of latitude. The very straightness of the boundary betrays its artificiality. One is reminded of the shapeless contour of Poland. A witty American who described South Dakota as the "state without end," might equally well have been referring to Canada.

"I remember some years ago," he wrote, "a friend explained to me that every time I went to the post office I crossed 45° north. I had not been aware of it. He pointed to the exact place, near a tree, and ever afterwards I found myself stepping high when I passed over the spot so as not to trip. But a state that must depend for its boundaries on such map-makers' devices is unfortunate." [1]

In Canada there is plenty of space. With her three and a half million square miles she is not conceived on the European plan. Her area, greater even than that of the United States owing to her immense northern wilderness, is typically American. Her enormous size is less noticeable in the east where the distances are still, to our way of thinking, reasonable enough; but

[1] *These United States*, p. 263 (T.I.).

in the west and north they are overwhelming. From Quebec to Vancouver is over 2500 miles, including 750 from Winnipeg to the Rockies, and 500 from Calgary to the Pacific Ocean; the distance from Quebec to the Labrador coast again is 750 miles, while from Lake Ontario to the Hudson Bay is almost 625, and from Edmonton to the Arctic Ocean 1250. The area of Canada is thirty times that of the British Isles and accounts for 27 per cent of the whole area of the British Empire.

The separate Canadian provinces, however, are about on the scale of the countries of Europe. Manitoba is twice the size of the British Isles; Ontario is equal to France and Germany together; and Quebec to France, Germany, and Spain. Such astronomical figures are hard to visualize. To appreciate them fully one must travel over these vast spaces.

Three and a half million square miles! As big as Europe. But let us not linger over statistics, for after all they are only theoretical, because the area of Canada that has so far been developed is relatively small. Owing either to the nature of the soil or to the climate, it will be impossible ever to make use of much of Canada's territory. A map of the density of the population [1] shows that the districts that have been effectively cultivated after three centuries of colonization and de-

---

[1] *See* Map on p. 56.

velopment, still amount only to a long thin strip glued to the American frontier. Although this strip spreads out on the western prairies, its width is strictly limited in the St. Lawrence Valley where it is hemmed in by the Laurentian Shield, whose rugged bluish horizon poetically marks the end, the northern limit of human habitation. Since her zone of occupation is extremely narrow, Canada is a state which lacks body. Therefore she is always tempted to seek a centre of gravity outside her own borders.

Yet in taking our inventory of Canada it would be quite wrong to consider the vast northern area as a liability, for, on the contrary, its existence constitutes a factor of great importance to the Canadian personality. Referring again to the symmetry between the American continents in the northern and southern hemispheres, Canada admittedly has its counterpart in the wheatlands of the Argentine, while British Columbia and Alaska correspond to Chile. But the great Northland, because of the peculiar shapes of the two continents, has only a puny counterpart in Patagonia. The Northland is thus peculiarly Canadian and the only Arctic country in either continent.

The effect of the North on the Canadian individuality is noteworthy. Its importance lies less in its economic value than in what one may term its mystic appeal. Many countries—and they are to be envied—

possess in one direction or another a window which opens out on to the infinite—on to the potential future. The open sky thus becomes part of their frontier, and to them it acquires a symbolical, almost a spiritual significance. In the United States it is the West; in Germany it is the East—that East where her genius for organization hopes to develop unfettered; in our Algeria it is the South, and in South Africa, in the heroic days of Cecil Rhodes, it was the North—"My North" as he passionately called it. In Canada the frontier which abounds in poetry and latent hopes is less the West, as in the United States, than the Northwest, or simply, the North. What an attraction it had for the pioneers, the backwoodsmen, the mining prospectors, and the missionaries! They all felt, and not without reason, that here was a land that was limitless. In these new countries people speak, with their eyes shining, of the "limitless possibilities," "the unbounded potentialities" that still await them. How often have I heard such expressions of hope in America and Australia!

No Canadian will ever disown the North, for to him it is a boundless territory of unknown possibilities. Doubtless it is some obscure instinct that makes him resent as a criticism any remark by a foreigner about the severity of these lands which in truth do demand the maximum of Man's energy. They have never forgiven Voltaire for referring to their country as "a few acres of snow," and many are still angry over the vigorous description of the rude life of the pioneers around Lake St. John given in *Maria Chapdelaine*. Yet the North is always there like a presence; it is the background of the picture without which Canada would not be Canada.

But the Canadian North must be considered from still another angle, as a link between the various continents. Terrestrial distances, of course, become shorter as we approach the Poles, and for this reason Canada finds herself particularly well placed to serve as an intercontinental or imperial highway. The Fathers of Confederation realized this in 1867, and so did the English statesmen from whom they received encouragement. Both were determined that this route between England, the Far East and Australia should remain entirely British. Modern posters advertising the Canadian Pacific Railway and its maritime services, "The C.P.R. Spans the World," express this same idea.

What is new, however, is the importance gained by the Northland through aviation. In future the most direct air route between America and Europe, or between America and Asia, will pass northwards over Canada. From the United States to England planes will travel by way of Labrador and Greenland; from the United States to Japan via Alaska, the best way will be across either British Columbia or the Canadian prairies east of the Rockies. In 1935, when an American squadron bound for Alaska alighted at Edmonton, the capital of Alberta suddenly realized that it was on the route to Asia.

It is a privilege for a country to be situated on a great international highway: a greater privilege, perhaps, not to be! But Canada cannot escape her destiny. Even today her government realizes not only its rights but its eventual responsibilities as an Arctic nation. As a matter of policy it must keep in constant contact with the North, right up to the Pole. This doctrine, though not recognized in principle by the United States, expresses an essential aspiration of the Canadian nation.

As far back as 1846, Disraeli, who was far ahead of his time, said in the House of Commons, "I am not one of those who believe that the destiny of Canada must inevitably be annexation with the United States. Canada possesses all the elements of a great independent country. It is destined, I sometimes say to myself, to become the Russia of the New World."

§ 2

Although Canada's problem is due in part to its continental and intercontinental location, it also arises from its geological structure, and from the position, in relation to one another, of its various regions. A detailed description of the geological structure hardly lies within the province of this study, still a brief reference to certain relatively simple characteristics is necessary, since they constitute an essential part of the country's personality.

When I look at a geological map, or simply recall my own personal experiences, what impresses me most is the enormous mass of the Laurentian Shield. This, the oldest geological unit in North America, is an intricate mass of granite and schists and metamorphosed sedimentary strata with many igneous intrusions of pre-Cambrian age all deeply eroded, reduced to a featureless plateau and finally subjected to intense glacial erosion in the last glacial period. The Laurentian Shield covers an area of 2,800,000 square miles and completely encircles Hudson Bay. It cuts diagonally across the northwest, and borders the northern shores of the Great Lakes and also the north side of the St. Lawrence Valley, and finally dominates the Gulf of St. Lawrence. North of Lake Superior the Laurentian Shield is over 300 miles wide, and it extends 600 miles east and west of Hudson Bay. It is always recognizable by its dark blue line of hills which blot out the horizon.

One is instinctively reminded of Sweden and Finland with their hard rocks, their meagre deposits of soil, their sheltered pools of brown water, and their endless forests. Such glaciated topography does not allow water to drain well, so there are innumerable

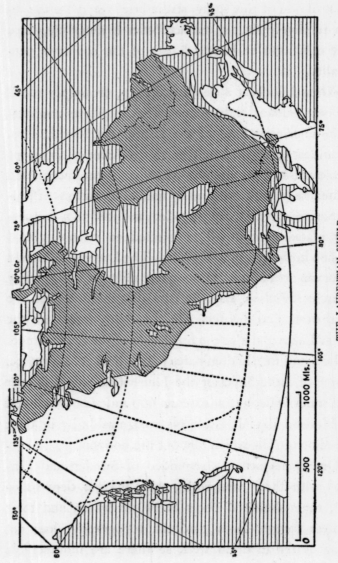

THE LAURENTIAN SHIELD

lakes. The rivers are alternately stagnant or broken by rapids, and therefore cannot be navigated except by Indian canoes. This intractable region is rich in mineral resources, and especially suitable for generating hydro-electric power. The twentieth century realizes this and will no doubt make better use of it than its predecessors have done.

The rough framework of the rest of the continent consists of two ridges. In the east the Appalachians run parallel to the Atlantic northeastwards from Alabama to Newfoundland. They join up with the Adirondacks, a small advance spur of the Laurentian Shield. Much more extensive and complex are the Rockies, which cover all of the extreme west of Canada. They are Tertiary and Palaeozoic on their eastern slopes. On their western side, where they form the Cascade range, they are Mesozoic.

In the centre, between these two ridges, lies the great plain narrowing towards the north between the converging slopes of the Laurentians and the Rockies. Thus the outstanding features which give the country its individuality are first the heavy mass of the Laurentian Shield, then the vastness of the prairies, and lastly the high relief of the mountain range which dominates them on their western side. With the exception of the Laurentians, which are essentially Canadian, the other regions are simply continuations of the United States, a fact which is of the utmost consequence, not only geo-graphically, but politically as well.

Because of the very nature of its geographic make-up, the Canadian climate lacks diversity. This is most important, as we shall see again when we study the economic aspect. We have here a country which is essentially continental, but which is much more influenced by the North Pole than by the Gulf of Mexico, or even by the neighbouring oceans. The warm Chinook winds from the south sometimes reach the prairies, but more often a bitter gale from the north seems to come straight from the Pole itself. It is remarkable how little the sea atmosphere penetrates inland. On the Pacific coast it does not pass beyond the first slopes of the Rockies, and as for the Atlantic, it actually influences Eastern Canada less than it, in its turn, is influenced by the mainland. The paradox is that when the ocean meets the Gulf of St. Lawrence it seems to assimilate the climate of the continent. In all these characteristics, Canada is more like Asia than Europe.

The various climatic zones are scarcely different from one another. This is because the climate, being continental rather than meridional, falls into vertical zones prolonging those of the United States. When I crossed Canada from the Pacific to the Atlantic in the month of February, I remember that a soft rain was falling on the west coast, but in the Rockies and on the prairies

38

the snow lay white on the ground under a brilliant sun. In Toronto it rained again owing to the mild humid influence of the Lakes, but when I reached Quebec there was snow and cold, and the St. Lawrence was full of ice. When I made the same journey in the opposite direction in the summer, from June to September, I recall a warm persistent rain in the east, grilling heat in the centre, then a fresh mountain breeze on the other side of the prairies, and finally, in Vancouver and Victoria, the mild weather of the Pacific.

The only region in which the atmosphere seemed to be influenced by the south was on the American frontier in the Rockies, where the climate of the high plateaux of Mexico, Arizona, and Utah seemed to have been projected northwards. These valleys reminded me more of the Atlas Mountains, however, than of the Alps. Everywhere else Canada was Nordic, almost Arctic. Therefore, unlike the United States, or even the Argentine, or Roumania (which she resembles in some ways), she can never be a country complete in herself. There can never be any question of an autonomous economy. To give her her due, she has achieved her independence, contrary to the dictates of geography itself.

The country thus falls naturally into several different regions. From east to west there are four good districts, separated from each other by undeveloped areas.

The Maritime Provinces, with their forests and mines and some fine agricultural land; then the St. Lawrence Valley, the seat of the first colonizations and still the main centre of Canadian civilization; then the western prairies, more recently colonized by wheat growers; and lastly British Columbia, a land of forests, mines, and fisheries, but clearly concerned with the attractions, preoccupations, and problems of the Pacific.

Interspersed between these regions, which have been particularly blessed by Nature, are three others which by contrast are mediocre and difficult to develop. The *hinterland* of the Maritimes, including Gaspé, is the first barrier. Then on the plateau north of Lake Superior and Lake Huron we find a scanty covering of trees, hard unyielding rocks, and a glaciated horizon which is the very synonym of sterility. Finally the Rocky Mountains, impressive in their grandeur and solitude, endowed with mineral wealth and magnificent for tourists, are devoid of population. Naturally the Far North must be classified apart, with its vast territories devoted to hunting, fishing, mining, adventure, missions. . . .

This brings us to the conclusion that there is bound to be lack of contact between the developed regions. Travelling by train from the Maritime Provinces of the Atlantic coast to Quebec takes 24 hours across an empty wilderness; from Toronto to Winnipeg requires 48 hours by rail over a rocky desert, sparsely sprinkled with trees but without soil or vegetation; from Calgary to Vancouver, another 24 hours, through magnificent country where one feels, however, that humanity has made only a precarious impression. Each of these regions, rich or poor, empty or populated, corresponds to an adjoining region in the United States, of which it is merely an extension. For this reason the Maritime Provinces are irresistibly attracted towards New England, the valley of the St. Lawrence towards New York, the prairies towards the American West, and British Columbia towards the American Pacific coast. Vancouver is more intimately connected with Seattle than with Quebec, St. John, N. B., with Boston rather than with Calgary. In spite of a political frontier, which in reality does not separate, there is something more here than mere resemblance and relationship. Geographically, the environment is the same; the people are the same, and the life is the same.

In the entire configuration one sees plainly something that might endanger the political unity of Canada. This unity is essentially based on the east-west axis which arises from a continuous movement in that direction of population, of colonization, of the railways, of confederation, and of the British or Imperial allegiance—it is part of the permanent relationship of Europe. But the attraction of the United States also provides a per-

petual orientation from north to south, owing to its
proximity, its resemblance, and its similarity of interests; all of which tend to compromise the political
unity of Canada.

The Canadian problem lies in the inherent contra-
diction of a country which is American in its geographical position, its physical nature, and its whole atmosphere, but whose political existence relies on an initial,
and so far unbroken, bond with England and Europe.
In this we recognize the two contrary axes of the New
World, and the struggle between history and geography
of which the Americas are the theatre. Nowhere is this
struggle so intense as in Canada, where it is at once a
source of weakness and of strength. The weakness is
that of a country which is hybrid and divided, and which
is not sure of itself. It is unable to choose between the
United States and England without destroying itself
in the process. Hence arises the uncertainty of a heterogeneous people, who are not sure they want the degree
of cultural unity that would be necessary for the definite
achievement of their personality.

But at the same time this weakness, which is caused
by the country's very complexity, also gives birth to
an undeniable strength. Canada is the only country in
America which has kept its political link with Europe,
and therefore it has an intimacy of its own with the
older civilizations on which is based the culture of all

the western world. Canada is American, but it is also British, and authentically French. Though it may be tempted to drift into a provincialism which has not spared the United States, it is compelled by its position in the Empire to be international. The role of interpreter, which its governments well know how to fill, raises it above its own level. From the point of view of Europe, it is useful to have in North America a distinct political individuality called Canada.

II

DEMOGRAPHY

CHAPTER III

POLITICS AND POPULATION

§ 1

WE have felt justified in saying that there is no geographical necessity for the existence of a special political unit called Canada. Nevertheless this political unit does exist. There is a Canadian state, a Canadian people, and a Canadian nation. History has been the determining factor—history, dominated by chance events without which it might have been entirely different. Let us now recall the essential stages of the territorial formation of Canada in so far as they have been inseparably linked with the development of her population.

The first period brings us to the end of the French domination, and to the independence of America. La Nouvelle France in the eighteenth century consisted of the whole of the St. Lawrence and Mississippi basins, while England possessed all the Atlantic coast from Alabama up to Newfoundland including Acadia, her sovereignty over the latter having been confirmed in 1713 by the Treaty of Utrecht. Rupert's Land in the Far North, which had been claimed by the Hudson's Bay Company since 1670, was only vaguely defined on the south and east. After French rule had been brought to an end by the Treaty of Paris in 1763, the English territory extended over the entire continent east of the Mississippi, except for Florida. The French population, which still remained on the banks of the St. Lawrence, obtained a treaty guaranteeing the protection of their language, their religion, and their land tenure. The rights accorded in this initial agreement are still maintained by their descendants, who realize that they are of prime importance to the status of the French Canadian population.

The British domain was soon curtailed when an independent American power was constituted. The Treaty of Versailles in 1783 liberated the former British colonies, which became the United States. It also demarcated a frontier which has remained practically unchanged ever since, and which extended between the U.S.A. and Canada from the Atlantic to the headwaters of the Mississippi. The British Canadian element, which was small in comparison with the French, was reinforced by the mass migration of the United Empire Loyalists. These were the Americans who, remaining faithful to the King of England, settled in Acadia, on the northern shore of Lake Ontario, and in the Eastern Townships not far from Montreal. The essential characteristics of Canada were thus constituted both by the distinct French population and by the arrival of this wave of "loyalists" to reinforce the small existing English population.

The second period extends from the American Revolution to the Canadian Confederation in 1867. The division of the country into Upper and Lower Canada by the Constitutional Act of 1791 recognized two distinct provinces, the one French on the east, and the other to the southwest of the Ottawa river. This separation, which arose from the racial structure of the map, was destined to last in spite of a temporary constitution from 1841 to 1867, when Upper and Lower Canada were united into a single province. The two provinces came into being again when Quebec and Ontario were formed at the time of the Confederation.

As the nineteenth century gradually came to its close, attention began to be directed towards the West. As early as 1825 a treaty had fixed the exact boundary between the Russian territory of Alaska and the Hudson's Bay Company's lands which were stretching farther and farther towards the west. By a series of equally important agreements from 1814 to 1846, the frontier between the United States and Canada was peaceably fixed along the 49th parallel of latitude. The British possessions now extended out to the Pacific. In 1849 the island of Vancouver was granted to the Hudson's Bay Company, but was surrendered in 1858 when it was constituted a Crown Colony (as it still remembers!). Also in 1858 the mainland opposite the island received the same status. The two colonies were united in 1866 when British Columbia was formed.

Meanwhile, the Maritime Provinces had also been steadily evolving. These territories had been acquired in 1713 by the Treaty of Utrecht. In 1720 Nova Scotia was created, and by 1758 it had its own legislature. Prince Edward Island was founded in 1768 and New Brunswick in 1786.

The only bond that these territories had in common was that they all belonged to England, for the political personality of Canada, although already present in the minds of her statesmen, still did not exist.

In 1867 the British North America Act, by uniting the provinces of Quebec, Ontario, New Brunswick and Nova Scotia in a single confederation, created the Dominion of Canada. The Northwest Territories were transferred in 1870 to the Confederation, to which was also added in the same year the newly-formed province of Manitoba. British Columbia in 1871 and Prince Edward Island in 1873 rallied in their turn to the Dominion, which was now complete. Since then only minor changes have been made in the boundaries, such as a rectification in Alaska in favour of the United States in 1903, and on the Labrador coast in favour of Newfoundland in 1927. Without this union, which became necessary on the morrow of the American Civil War, the British colonies, scattered from the Atlantic to the Pacific, would not have resisted the latent menace of absorption by their powerful neighbour.

In 1867 the task of organizing the great unexplored regions still remained to be done, and so far it has already absorbed three generations of patient effort. In 1880 Canada inherited the English claim to the islands of the Arctic, and in 1882, detaching themselves from the Northwest Territories, the districts of Saskatchewan, Assiniboia, Alberta, and Athabaska set themselves up as distinct administrative units. Twenty-three years later Saskatchewan and Assiniboia on the one hand, and Alberta and Athabaska on the other, became the present autonomous provinces of Saskatchewan and Alberta, and in 1912 Manitoba, Ontario, and Quebec were considerably enlarged. In 1898 Yukon Territory was created, and in 1918 the remainder of the enormous Northwest was divided into three territories, Franklin, Keewatin, and Mackenzie.[1]

This complicated territorial development showed an unwavering determination to create a unified British community stretching from ocean to ocean, and to keep it distinct from the United States. During this period of construction, politics held the forces of geography in leash. The Canadian Pacific Railway, promised to

[1] For further geographical data see *An Historical Atlas of Canada*, by Lawrence J. Burpee (Thomas Nelson & Sons Ltd.), 1927.

British Columbia in order to induce her to join the Confederation, established Canada on an axis running from east to west. Without the transcontinental railway, which was essential to the very existence of the Dominion, the north-south tendency would certainly have prevailed, breaking up the country into isolated sections, which sooner or later would have joined the United States. We must not, even yet, regard the matter as definitely settled. If the desire for a united Canada, which is strong among the leaders but very slight in certain provinces, were to weaken, the latent attraction towards the south would immediately reassert itself. It is a question of desire and it varies according to the composition of the different parts of the population.

§ 2

When the last census of Canada was made in 1931, it was found that the population had risen to 10,376,786 inhabitants. In 1871, when the first census of the Confederation was made, the figure was only 3,689,257, and in 1901 on the eve of the great development of the West it amounted to 5,371,315. Thus we have an immense territory with a relatively sparse population amounting to an average of no more than 2.99 inhabitants per square mile. This calculation is, of course, mere theory, since it includes the whole of the empty North. Yet even in the districts which have been effectively developed, the population numbers are extraordinarily small.

As I have already noted, the populated parts of Canada are still relatively limited and consist of a narrow band along the American frontier. There are, it is true, two fairly dense zones with at least 25 inhabitants per square mile and often many more—I mean first the districts north of Lake Ontario and Lake Erie, and secondly the valley of the St. Lawrence. There are also a few areas in the Maritime Province with a fair density. Then comes four zones with a population of less than 25 inhabitants per square mile: up-country in the Maritime Provinces, the few parts of northern Ontario and Quebec which have been colonized, the western prairies, and, in British Columbia, the coast and a few valleys. The rest, as Shakespeare says, is silence!

The following table of provincial populations gives an authoritative review of the demography of the country: [1]

	Inhabitants	Per Cent of Dominion Total
Maritime Provinces	1,009,103	9.73
Ontario and Quebec	6,305,938	60.77
Western Provinces	2,353,529	22.68
British Columbia	694,263	6.69
Yukon and Northwest	13,953	.13

[1] All the statistics given in this book are (unless otherwise stated) obtained from the *Canada Year Book*, published annually by the Dominion Bureau of Statistics.

The centre of gravity thus lies decidedly to the East, since the five provinces of Ontario, Quebec, Nova Scotia, New Brunswick and Prince Edward Island contain over two-thirds of the population.

The West, including British Columbia, constitutes a minority of less than 30 per cent, and the North practically nothing. However, the proportion of the West in the total has steadily increased, up to 1931 at any rate, while that of the East has diminished. Between 1871 and 1931, the Maritime Provinces fell from about 21 per cent of the total to 10 per cent, and Ontario and Quebec from 76 per cent to 60 per cent, while the West jumped from 3 per cent to nearly 30 per cent, as quoted above. Population has been thus accumulating along an East-West line following the transcontinental railways. Up to 1881, the "centre of population" was no farther west than Valleyfield in the Province of Quebec: by 1901 it had moved as far as Pembroke, Ontario, and in 1931 it was situated near Lake Superior, a little to the north of Sault Ste. Marie. Up to 1911 this movement indicated a trend towards the northwest, but it was deflected due westwards after 1921, and in the present decade it will probably again be found to have moved northwards.

The greatest development of the population took place at the beginning of the twentieth century, from 1900 to 1914. While the increase made in the decade,

1891-1901, was 11 per cent, in the following decade, 1901-1911, it rose to 34 per cent, which in its turn was followed by 22 per cent from 1911 to 1921, and 18 per cent from 1921 to1931. In the space of thirty years the population of the three prairie provinces rose from 419,512 inhabitants in 1901 to 1,956,082 in 1921, and to 2,353,529 in 1931.

The way for such rapid expansion was prepared first by the cession to the Dominion in 1870 of the vast un-developed territories of the Northwest, and secondly by the completion in 1886 of the Canadian Pacific Rail-way, which opened up new lands for colonization. Also, as the American West was beginning to fill up, the "last best west" alive with possibilities, was now in Canada. The heavy immigration of the first fourteen years of the twentieth century, which, in one year on the eve of the war reached the figure of almost 400,000, pro-vided an ever-increasing army ready to develop the country. To this development of the West must be added the industrial expansion of the East during the same period, and also the influx of British capital up to the war, with an even greater volume from the United States in the post-war years. It is not surprising that under such favourable circumstances people felt that Canada's steady progress would go on unchecked.

If we consider, not the development of the country,

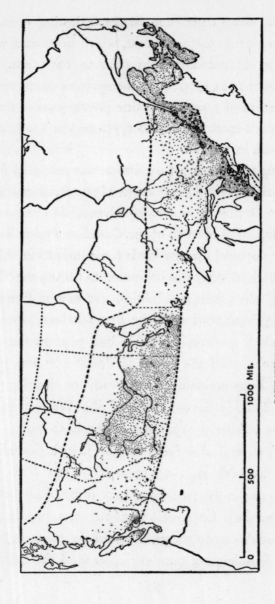

DISTRIBUTION OF POPULATION : CENSUS 1931

---------- line north of which prospecting is practically non-existent, except along certain rivers

but the actual volume of its effective population, then we must admit that it is still mediocre and unsubstantial. Although certain regions, such as the St. Lawrence Valley, are well populated—paradoxically enough even over-populated—others, like the West and British Columbia, are still only superficially occupied. But the West is rich. It should be colonized by the East, and the latter could direct towards those great empty but promising spaces the excess of population from the regions which are already full, and where the birth-rate is high. History, however, shows that the competing appeal of the South is dangerously powerful. The Canadians of the East, crossing a very near frontier, feel more at home in the factories of New England than in the far-off atmosphere of the prairies. This centrifugal attraction is a peril which, if it is to be overcome, requires unceasing vigilance.

The obvious consequence of a sparse population in the existing economic order is that Canada's products, which with such resources naturally are abundant, cannot find a sufficient internal market, and so must be exported. The country cannot, therefore, form an economic unit, closed if need be, like the United States. And so the economic attraction of its great neighbour is as irresistible as if the universal law of gravity also operates mathematically in the world of trade. In discussing the Dominion's relations with the United States one must always bear in mind the map of her population.

§ 3

Hitherto we have dealt with the numbers rather than with the composition of the population. Now Canada is not homogeneous, either demographically or racially.

As a rule we do not study nearly enough the demographic age of a country. It is not the same in the long-established populations of Eastern Canada as it is in the West, where they are newer and still in process of evolution. The coefficient of masculinity—the proportion of men to women—is always interesting, for it discloses fairly accurately the degree of the social evolution of a people, old countries having more women, and young countries more men. In 1931 there were in the entire population of Canada 107 men to 100 women, or an excess of males of 3.59 per cent. In the whole of Europe, with the exception of Bulgaria and Ireland, there are more women than men. It is significant that the entire New World reveals a contrary situation. The excess of males in the Argentine, for example, is 6.57 per cent, and in the United States, 1.22 per cent. Judged by this measure, Canada must be classed among the younger countries.

Oddly enough the Canadian population has become more marked in its masculinity since the end of the

nineteenth century, which is tantamount to saying that
it has become rejuvenated.

Year	Men per 100 Women
1871	102
1881	101
1891	103
1901	105
1911	111
1921	106
1931	107

The great movement of immigration, which began
in 1900 and naturally brought an excess of men into
the country, explains this evolution, which has varied
in intensity from one decade to another. A new Canada
was born in the West after the completion of the Canadian Pacific Railway, as is clearly shown in the following table of the masculine coefficient of the various
provinces in the year 1931:

Province	Men per 100 Women
Prince Edward Island	106
Nova Scotia	105
New Brunswick	104
Quebec	101
Ontario	104
Manitoba	110
Saskatchewan	118
Alberta	120
British Columbia	124
Northwest Territories	115
Yukon	201

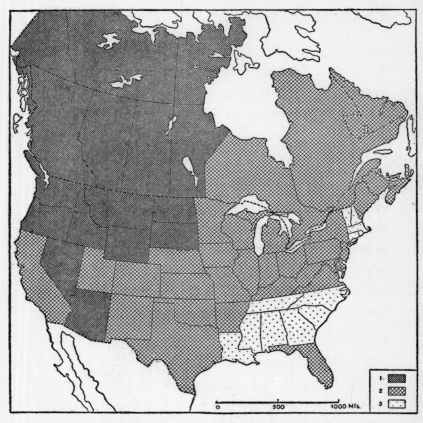

PROPORTION OF MEN TO WOMEN IN CANADA AND THE UNITED STATES
(BY PROVINCES OR STATES)

1. More than 110 men to 100 women
2. Between 100 to 110 men to 100 women
3. More women than men

In the East the population is well established, notably in the Province of Quebec, where since 1763 the
French element has not been increased by immigration, but simply by its own vigorous birth-rate. In the
West, on the contrary, where the population is still in
process of formation, the equilibrium towards which
the two sexes are naturally tending has not yet had time
to find its proper level. This phenomenon is true not
only of Canada, for if we tabulate the populations of
even a few of the American states on the 1931 basis,
we discover the same result:

State	Men per 100 Women
Massachusetts	95
South Carolina	95
Georgia	97
Illinois	103
North Dakota	112
Montana	120
Nevada	140

These figures manifestly reveal a situation parallel
to that of Canada, although the latter developed a generation later.

When we come to study racial origin we find everywhere this same lack of homogeneity. The Canadian
people bear the mark of their initial political formation
today, just as they did a hundred years ago. After she
became British, Canada was not able to absorb the
French group, and the English element, increased by

61

the "Loyalists," simply settled alongside, without assimilating or making any impression upon it. Although the recent cosmopolitan immigration into the West is adapting itself to the Canadian type, that does not necessarily mean that it is becoming British. As a matter of fact the American people are no less composite, but there one finds a definite effort to assimilate all newcomers, whoever they may be. The French Canadians, on the other hand, enjoy special treaty rights and as they are determined to remain a distinct race, they constitute a block which is not amenable to unification. Furthermore, in the United States the policy of assimilation is exerted in favour of a definite civilization which is at once Anglo-Saxon and American, and no alternative is possible. In Canada one finds competition between a French Canadian civilization maintaining its own individuality, a British civilization enjoying the prestige of England, and an American civilization turning for its example, its basis, and its very being, to the powerful southern neighbour.

Thus Canadian nationality undoubtedly is a problem. It exists, but if it is to persist it is essential that all Canadians, whatever their tradition, must be, first and foremost, Canadians. Now even in my own acquaintance are some who are "French Canadians," not simply "Canadians." I know others whose culture is so completely American that any hope of a national personality of their own seems to be out of the question. Others again have remained so purely English that their British reactions come before their strictly Canadian reactions. Finally, in British Columbia and, strange as it seems, among certain French Canadians in Quebec, there are those who regret the colonial regime, and who, in their heart of hearts are tempted to place more confidence in the government at London than in the one at Ottawa. Such British rather than imperial sentiments are becoming rarer, but to some extent they still retard the full bloom of a national Canadian consciousness.

CHAPTER IV

THE FRENCH ELEMENT

§ 1

In Canada in 1931, out of a total of 10,376,786 inhabitants, 2,927,990 were French Canadians. Those of British origin numbered 5,381,071, which leaves only 2,067,725 belonging to other races such as Continental European, Negroid, American Indian and Asiatic.[1] These figures emphasize the relative importance of the French group.

The French Canadians are descended entirely from the 65,000 French from the western departments of France (Ile de France, Normandy, Maine, Anjou, Charente, Brittany), who were abandoned on the banks of the St. Lawrence by the Treaty of Paris in 1763. Cut off from intercourse with France from whom they received no further reinforcements, their only hope of survival lay in their own vitality. That, as we see, has not failed them, for these millions of French, relying on their own resources, have written in the New World an astonishing page of history. Their old mother coun-

---

[1] In Canadian population and immigration statistics there is no heading for "American" origin. Immigrants from the U.S.A. are subdivided into the original European or other racial stocks.

try forgot them for over a hundred years, though it is true in 1855 the frigate *La Capricieuse* made a famous and quite exceptional visit. Then, towards the end of the nineteenth century, she suddenly rediscovered them, and has since maintained a passionate interest which has never wavered.

A map of the French Canadian population reveals two principal groups: one in the Province of Quebec, overflowing on the west into Ontario, and the other in the Maritime Provinces, particularly in New Brunswick. Secondary groups, less compact but constituting important minorities, are found partly in Ontario in the neighbourhood of Detroit, partly north of the Great Lakes around Sault Ste. Marie and in the Temiskaming district, and finally, a few scattered over the western prairies, with small concentrations in Winnipeg and Edmonton. Although numerically small, we must add those of the Far North where French Canadians, both whites and half-breeds, are met with everywhere from the Atlantic to the Rockies.

The French population, taken by provinces, is as follows:

	Total Population	French Canadians	Per Cent
Maritime Provinces	1,009,000	207,000	20
Quebec	2,874,000	2,270,000	72
Ontario	3,432,000	300,000	8
Prairie Provinces	2,353,000	136,000	5
British Columbia	694,000	15,000	2

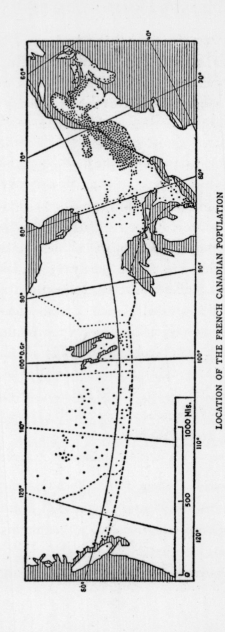

LOCATION OF THE FRENCH CANADIAN POPULATION

The stages of the vigorous French Canadian development are easily traced. In the St. Lawrence Valley, the original theatre of their occupation, their prolific birthrate caused them to spread out like a drop of oil. They first captured practically the entire Province of Quebec, and they then began to overflow into the neighbouring Province of Ontario. In 1901 only five counties remained in Quebec with an English majority: Argenteuil, Brome, Huntingdon, Pontiac, and Stanstead; by 1931 they were reduced to three: Brome, where the French account for 45 per cent, Huntingdon 48 per cent, and Pontiac 40 per cent. In the farm lands of the St. Lawrence Valley below Montreal, the French Canadian majorities usually attain 95 per cent and even higher: 98 per cent in the county of Beauce and 99 per cent in Bagot. In the Montreal area including the City of Montreal, out of a total of 1,020,000 inhabitants, 620,000 or 60 per cent are French. In the area about Quebec City the proportion is much higher: 157,000 French out of 171,000 inhabitants, or 91 per cent.

Their peaceful conquest of Eastern Ontario is not less striking. In the four eastern counties of Prescott, Glengarry, Stormont, and Russell, although in 1881 the French Canadians amounted to only 32,600 souls out of 93,358, or 35 per cent, they attained by 1901 51,935 out of 111,374 or 46 per cent, and in 1931 65,555 out of 119,617 or 54 per cent (in Prescott they amount to 79 per cent).

Similarly in New Brunswick (where they are called Acadians), their biological pressure seems to be irresistible:

Date	Total	Acadians	Per Cent
1871	285,594	44,907	16
1911	351,889	98,611	28
1931	408,219	136,999	33

A second stage of their development consisted in colonizing territories which are near by but not adjoining, such as the district around Lake St. John which they opened up at the end of the nineteenth century. The districts of Abitibi (88 per cent), Temiskaming (72 per cent), and Nipissing (45 per cent), all on the boundary between Quebec and Ontario, represent a more recent example of the same colonization.

A third stage, contemporary with the second one, carried the French Canadians into the West when that part of the country was being developed. Conditions here were not the same, for there was no direct contact between Quebec and the prairies. The colonists from the shores of the St. Lawrence, who went out to settle these new lands which differed so entirely from the country they had hitherto cleared and developed, were on the same footing as the mass of immigrants from Europe or the United States. They did not have the benefit, as they had had at Lake St. John or Abitibi, of a near-by starting point. Many of them actually arrived in the West by way of the United States. For this reason their settlements were sporadic, but they never dispersed, and their colonies always retained a certain individuality. Gradually the French population has ceased to be a local phenomenon limited to the Eastern Provinces.

Government statistics give us the exact numerical position of the French element, which in 1931 represented 28.22 per cent of the total population. It is concentrated in a massive block in the Province of Quebec, where it amounts to 79 per cent of the total population. Indeed, in the countryside of Quebec it is almost the whole population. Of the 2,927,990 French Canadians, 88 per cent belong to the St. Lawrence group, 7 per cent to the Maritime Provinces, and 5 per cent to the West. Expressed in cold figures, their development has been remarkable, as is disclosed in the following table:

French Canadian Population

	Total	Approx. Increase
1763	65,000	
1871	1,082,940	
1881	1,298,929	216,000

	Total	Approx. Increase
1891 [1]		
1901	1,649,371	350,000
1911	2,054,890	406,000
1921	2,452,743	398,000
1931	2,927,990	475,000

Although they have increased almost threefold in numbers, their proportion has declined slightly in relation to the total population of Canada:

Date	Per Cent
1871	31.07
1881	30.05
1901	30.71
1911	28.51
1921	27.91
1931	28.22

Nevertheless, if we consider each region separately, we find that the French element in both Quebec and New Brunswick is certainly tending to consolidate the positions won.

§ 2

What are the factors which have enabled this race, apparently doomed to disappear at the time of the Treaty of Paris, to develop and prosper?

The first assuredly is religion, which has maintained the French Catholics distinct from the English Protestants. This difference in religion is vital, for it expresses

[1] A separate census of the French Canadians was not taken in 1891.

the contrast between two civilizations, two traditions and two conceptions of life. The French population and the Catholic community do not of course coincide exactly, for as the French amount to only about 28 per cent of the total population and the Catholics to 41 per cent, there is obviously a margin of non-French Catholics. The French Canadians are practically all Catholics, the proportion being 97 per cent over the whole country, and reaching 99 per cent in the Province of Quebec.

There is no gainsaying the fact that the primary role in the preservation of the French Canadian tradition has been played by the Church. The priest, by preserving and guaranteeing the idea of the "family," has constituted a most effective bulwark for this little people, and has protected them from the risk of disintegration. It is he who, now as in the past, holds them together, physically and morally, and gives them the true conception of their own racial and spiritual individuality. The French Catholic of Canada no doubt is Canadian, but he is different from other Canadians. One may also say that he is American, in the sense that he belongs to the New World, but he must not be confused with the Catholic of the United States.

In addition to this religious bond, there is also among the French Canadians a purely racial consciousness. I wonder if it alone would be sufficient to assure the cohesion of the race! The most important influence exerted by the Church lies in education, which, from the primary to the superior schools, and even to the universities, is entirely in its hands. Above all it maintains its spiritual discipline over every phase of the life of the people, be it private or family, social, political, or economic. No aspect of their existence escapes its control. This priestly supervision has been able to be effective for so long a time only because it has kept the French Canadians completely immune from external influence. They have been kept free from contact with any ideas which might be considered dangerous germs. If one agrees to the aim in view, then this course is the essence of wisdom. If any intimacy, however slight, is allowed to develop with circles where the American spirit flourishes, the work of centuries may be endangered. We are forced to conclude that, without their priests, the French Canadians could not have remained intact—in other words they would not have survived.

Their use of the French language is the outstanding symbol of their unity. If it is to continue it must be taught in the schools as the principal language. In the Province of Quebec this is guaranteed by the Treaty of 1763 and is never questioned. In the English-speaking provinces the establishment of separate schools in which French is the principal tongue has met with obstinate ill will. However, the present tendency is for an agreement to be finally reached that French, even if it is not to continue as the principal language, shall at least be taught in the infant classes for a few years before English commences. This meets the essential difficulty, for, as the twig is bent so will it grow.

This educational policy can be carried out only where the community is sufficiently important to stand alone. Elsewhere there is little hope, especially for isolated cases, for experience proves that these are rapidly engulfed in their Anglo-Saxon surroundings. They are all the more vulnerable as the language they use professionally in the factory or office is English. It is not usually realized that not more than 3.5 per cent of English Canadians speak French, while 35 per cent of the French are bilingual. They learn English because they need it in business.

In addition to the temptation to abandon French, there is also the permanent danger of the language being corrupted. The French Canadians speak a good provincial French, which has stood the test of time, and has been considerably purified and improved during the past thirty years. The peasants speak an authentic country dialect, with a hint of the past, whereas cultivated circles speak most correctly, though in the towns anglicism is creeping in. It is with pleasure that we listen to picturesque old-fashioned expressions like the following, which reveal a desire to avoid English corruption:

Le char, instead of *le train*
Le petit char, instead of *le tramway*
L'engin, instead of *la locomotive*
Les lisses, instead of *les rails*
L'orateur, instead of *le president*
Le fourgon à boyaux, instead of *la pompe à incendie*
Les erreurs clericales, instead of *les fautes d'impression*

But unfortunately there are others, shameless camouflages of English which sound rather shocking:

Le char à steam, for *machine à vapeur*
La job, for *l'emploi*
La plume fontaine, for *le stylo*
Le watcher, for *l'observer*

The invasion is becoming irresistible in technical language, in sports and on the cinema. The continental atmosphere, which is American rather than English, threatens to impregnate everything, making it difficult for any but the well-educated to maintain the tradition of pure French correctly spoken.

If pure French is to continue, it will be because it is employed by the Church, in the sermon, in the confession, and in the daily activities of the parish, for otherwise it risks being corrupted even in family life. The priest, in a word, should be French-speaking. At first sight this problem may seem simple, for obviously the French Canadian priest is passionately devoted to the language, well knowing that it constitutes the first line in his system of defence.

True, but the Church, being a universal institution, does not feel that the language of Catholics should necessarily be French. On the contrary she may consider that, in North America, English represents the most effective means of spiritual communication, since it is spoken by over 95 per cent of the population. Without having the slightest hostility towards the French language in those parts where it is generally spoken, she may impose definite limits to its expansion, since one-third of the Canadian Catholics use the English tongue. Naturally no difficulty arises when a French-speaking ecclesiastic is chosen in the Province of Quebec, since no alternative is ever suggested. When a priest or a bishop has to be appointed to a parish or a diocese situated on a linguistic borderland, the problem becomes singularly delicate, all the more so as the choice may in the end cause the anglicizing or frenchifying of the district in question.

Thus, whether they wish it or not, the ecclesiastical authorities are dragged into politics. Bitter quarrels arise, far exceeding in gravity the point at issue, and usually disclosing local rivalry between the Irish and the French, as well as the need for the Church to allocate separate zones of influence for each of the two languages.

A little trick, which really settles nothing, consists in appearing to give satisfaction to the French Canadian element of some diocese by sending them as bishop a Mgr. Dupont (as we shall call him), who, however, does not speak French. Somewhere else the Church tries to appease the opposite camp by appointing a Mgr. Fraser (shall we say), a pure French Canadian in spite of his name! This by-play is important, for the future of the diocese is at stake.

It is interesting to show the situation in some of the Ontario dioceses where disputes have arisen:

Diocese	Percentage of French Canadians in Catholic Population	Bishop	Nationality
Haylebury	76	Mgr. Rheaume	French Canadian
Alexandria	71	Mgr. Couturier	English
Ottawa	76	Mgr. Forbes	French Canadian
Northern Ontario	60	Mgr. Hallé	French Canadian
Pembroke	50	Mgr. Ryan	Irish
Sault Ste. Marie	48	Mgr. Dignan	Irish
London	36	Mgr. Kidd	English
Toronto	11	Mgr. McGuigan	Scottish
Peterborough	18	Mgr. O'Connor	Irish
Kingston	17	Mgr. Spratt	Irish
Hamilton	4	Mgr. McNally	Irish

The final decision in the appointment of bishops is made outside the Canadian boundaries by the authorities at Rome, who have the right to say how far, from the religious point of view, the domain of the French language should extend. The Holy See appears inclined to leave to the French their present territory, but does not seem disposed to allow them any increase in an English-speaking North America. The Church refuses to identify itself completely with the small minority who speak the French tongue.

The French Canadians have been allowed to survive thanks to their religion and their language, but it is owing to their birth-rate that they have increased in such prodigious proportions. In spite of an inevitable tendency to decline, the birth-rate in the Province of Quebec, traditionally enormous, is still high. It was 80 per 1000 in 1765, and as high as 40 in 1875. Since then it has dropped to 37 in 1913, 33 in 1925, and 25 in 1934. Actually the real level is higher than this, for these statistics include the English minority. The French birth-rate is over 30 per 1000 in many counties, especially in recently colonized districts. Contrary to expectations, it has not declined much in the big cities, remaining at 20 in Montreal and 28 in Quebec, in 1933. Therefore, even today the French Canadians are still prolific—at least such is a foreigner's impression. Big families even in the towns seem to be the rule, in contrast to the small families of the English, and especially of the Americans.

This fecundity was offset in the nineteenth century by an exceptionally high death-rate, amounting until 1897 to over 20 per 1000. Since then an efficient effort has been made to introduce more hygienic conditions, and as a result this figure declined to 17 in 1920 and to 10 in 1934, so that in spite of the falling birth-rate the rate of survival remains at 15 per 1000, which is considerable. This accounts for the increase of about 475,000 in the French Canadian population in the decade of 1921-31.

This phenomenon cannot be appreciated unless it is compared with the statistics of the other races in Canada:

1934	Birth-rate per 1000	Death-rate per 1000	Survival Rate per 1000
Entire Country	20.5	9.4	11.1
Quebec	25.3	10.6	14.7
Ontario	17.5	9.9	7.6
British Columbia	13.5	8.8	4.7

As this table shows, the birth-rate is low in the English community of Ontario, and lower still in British Columbia which is strongly influenced by the United States. The French Canadian increase is thus impressive, and would have very important consequences in the future if these were the only factors to be reckoned with. Nevertheless, such persistent fecundity in the present century, and especially on a continent where birth control has become the rule, is very important.

Will it last? For the answer we must find out why it has lasted up to the present. The first reason is that the Church takes a firm attitude against birth control, and its instructions, given through the confessional and enforced by rigorous penances, are generally followed. Secondly it is worthy of note that in a new country people do have large families. Here they feel that there will be no difficulty in establishing their children when they grow up, in the near-by city, in the United States, in the West, or in the regions of the North that will be opened up by that time. Perhaps local tradition is also important; at any rate it is the custom to have big families, and so it continues. Yet in spite of all this reasoning, the underlying tendency of the continent leads to biological sterility, and this influence may prove too strong. The lead of the French Canadians is, however, undisputed, and, even with a lower birth-rate, it is likely to continue.

Finally, I feel that the vitality of the French Canadian community is the result of a certain attitude towards life and work, which is found nowhere else in America. This is a Catholic conception, and is linked up with various traditions inherited from old-time France. It takes the form of a moral discipline of the

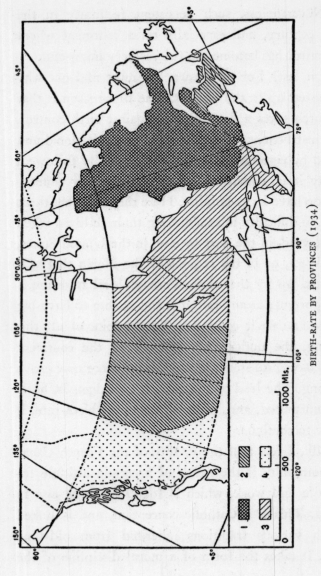

BIRTH-RATE BY PROVINCES (1934)

1. Very high : over 25 births per 1000 inhabitants
2. High : between 20 and 25 births per 1000 inhabitants
3. Average : between 15 and 20 births per 1000 inhabitants
4. Low : under 15 births per 1000 inhabitants

1000 Mls.

500

0

1   2   3   4

family, exerted under the direct influence of the Church. Thus it respects values which are considered out of date elsewhere, especially in the New World. It believes in hard work, commends thrift and self-discipline, accepts the doctrine of large families as a Christian duty, and restricts ambition to sensible proportions. Such thoughtful asceticism is the very negation of Americanism. Its principles are contrary to the underlying inspiration of the American civilization, even in its Catholic form. No compromise is possible, and if we dare look at the matter frankly we must admit that any assimilation by the French Canadians of American customs would mean the complete abandonment of their own traditions. They will survive only in so far as they refuse to be Americanized. The existence on the North American continent of a distinct people, ethnically different from their surroundings, is a curious paradox. Again one wonders if it can possibly last.

§ 3

If the birth-rate, the death-rate, and the rate of survival were the only things to be considered, the biological success of the French Canadians would be assured. But the question is more complex. There are other factors which determine the future of the Canadian people as a whole, and the fine asset side of the French position has a correspondingly heavy liability side as well. The disadvantage of the very strong defensive position that we have outlined is that clerical discipline is dearly paid for. As a result of the circumstances, and because the Church believes that it is working for the salvation of the race which has been entrusted to its care, it has assumed functions which are excessive and abnormal, yet which it is unwilling to relinquish. The Church, like certain parents, finds it hard to admit that its spiritual children, being now full-grown, are emancipating themselves. The priest tolerates no independence. If any activity arises outside of his sphere, he insinuates himself into it and imposes his will, or else prevents it from becoming effective. Even today it is not easy for a French Canadian to exist if he has incurred the ill-will of the ecclesiastical authorities, as has been proved by recent examples in literature and the Press. The Church instinctively tries to absorb the flower of the race by intensive recruiting, and so makes it difficult for any culture to develop beyond its jurisdiction. Now if the French Canadian civilization is to be complete, it must build up a culture of its own, and not rely solely on a Catholic culture; the nuance is important.

The birth-rate, which it is the custom to applaud, also exacts a heavy penalty. For many generations it has been accompanied by a correspondingly high death-rate, especially among new-born babies. These two phenomena are closely linked together, and probably the recent progress in reducing the death-rate will result in a reduction in the number of births. The stamina of the race no doubt will be improved—at the present time in the country districts the people are sturdy and capable of magnificent pioneering efforts, but in the cities they are showing signs of weakening. Owing to the custom of having large families it has been difficult to assure satisfactory hygienic conditions. When a woman has already borne twenty children, how can she possibly have sufficient vitality left to give birth to more who will be healthy?

There has been considerable improvement in the past few years, but previously, in excessively prolific families, not enough care was given to bodily health, especially as the people were influenced by the ecclesiastical tradition of not paying too much attention to the body. The natural consequence of this variety of circumstances and excessive fertility has been to maintain a lower standard of living in comparison with that of English Canadians. We admire these "fine families" in France, but we must not overlook the fact that in English-speaking circles in America they are an object of commiseration, and are regarded as the sign of an inferior civilization.

In the light of the above observations, one easily discerns the perils which may threaten the future of the

DEMOGRAPHY

French Canadian race. The most serious seems to me
to be the complete change in character which is sure
to result from the fact that this formerly rural people
is now largely urban. In the Province of Quebec, the
countryside in 1871 still contained 80.5 per cent of the
total population, but this proportion has now fallen to
37 per cent. This movement is general, but is most
accentuated on the shores of the St. Lawrence. It is
evident that, as a result, the French Canadians risk
losing their traditional qualities, for these were indis-
solubly linked up with the peasant life they are now
abandoning.

In the cities Americanization lies in wait, ready to
seize them. Once they have been enticed into the American atmosphere of movement and noise, so different
from that in which their ancestors were bred, how can
they hope to resist? When this proletariat has been
completely severed from the soil and transplanted to
an urban setting exactly like the U.S.A., it will lack
those reserves of spiritual nourishment which formerly
provided its racial defence. The appeal of standardized
comfort will prove irresistible. I do not suggest that
these masses will cease to be French. They can continue
to speak the French language, corrupted with anglicisms
perhaps, but in spirit they will have difficulty in remaining distinct.

A second danger appears in the migratory movements

which may diminish the French in numbers, or possibly increase their racial rivals. Owing to its high birth-rate, the Province of Quebec is always menaced by overpopulation, so the excess is obliged to go elsewhere. The important thing is that it should not be lost. If it flows towards the large Canadian cities, the result may be, as we have suggested, a loss in quality, but that is all. After all, the liberal professions must be recruited, and experience shows that the villages furnish talent of the first order. Again, if those who are leaving go out to colonize the West or the Far North, there is nothing in this solution of the problem to hinder the national development of the French. On the contrary, it is to such united groups of settlers that we owe the opening up of the districts of Lake St. John, Abitibi, Temiskaming, and others farther afield in the Northwest, but always in Canada. The Province of Quebec, following a most enlightened policy, organizes and then subsidizes this type of migration.

Such has not always been the case, however. In the past, when the son left his home in the village, more often than not the line of least resistance counselled him to direct his steps towards the United States. The life of the pioneer, especially in the North, was hard. How much more tempting was the prospect across the border, in a country very like his own with work at higher wages! In the latter half of the nineteenth century, when the New England cotton industry was developing most rapidly, it drew a large part of its requirements of factory labour from the Quebec countryside. At this time the French Canadians in their hundreds of thousands established themselves in Massachusetts, Rhode Island, and Connecticut, with no thought of returning. According to American statistics there were 371,000 immigrants whose parents had been born in Canada. The total Franco-American population amounted to about a million, though some even put at the two million mark the number of Americans of French Canadian origin throughout the United States. How much better for the French Canadian group if these *émigrés* had remained in their own country!

This French Canadian haemorrhage is only one aspect of the question. While the French are losing part of their population through emigration, with no hope of being able to make good the loss from elsewhere, the English-speaking element can, on the contrary, augment itself by immigration. So long as the settlers come from the British Isles this goes without saying, but even with immigrants from other sources the result is the same, for in the end assimilation always works in favour of the Anglo-Saxon race. The advantage which the French Canadians owe to their high birthrate can thus be counterbalanced. This was proved when their percentage declined owing to the intensive development of the West in the early years of the century.

The British majority might be tempted to overwhelm the French Canadian minority not merely by their own British numbers, but also by "packing the house" with immigrants, as the result of reopening the country to immigration. This eventuality, improbable as it may seem, leads us to an enlargement of the discussion. Let us examine the other elements that make up the Canadian population.

CHAPTER V

THE ENGLISH CANADIANS

§ 1

THE English Canadians in 1931 numbered 5,381,071 out of a total of 10,376,786 inhabitants.

They are of three different origins. First, those who came overseas from the British Isles, such as the Scots who arrived in Nova Scotia before the fall of Quebec, and the English, Irish, and Scottish who settled in the St. Lawrence Valley after the Treaty of Paris, and since then all over the country. Then, secondly, those who came from the United States, the great influx of United Empire Loyalists who settled in the Maritime Provinces, the eastern townships in Quebec, and at Kingston, Ontario. Finally, separate mention should be made of the intensely English groups which the English garrisons left behind them at Halifax and Victoria. These cities, still filled today with retired officers and their descendants, are imbued with the true "Colonial" spirit.

The difference between the English and French Canadians, is that the former have never lost contact with their homeland. from which they continue to receive reinforcements. The bond, moreover, is not merely demographic, but also social, religious, and political. In their new surroundings many of them are as English as ever in sentiment; in fact one cannot be sure at first sight if one is speaking to a Canadian of English stock, or to an Englishman who has recently settled in Canada. On the morrow of the American secession, England expected a rupture would come within the next few generations, but it has never taken place.

Geographically the British domain is as follows:

The Maritime Provinces (except the north of New Brunswick);

Ontario (except the counties bordering on Quebec);

Western Quebec (especially a part of Montreal and a part of the eastern townships);

The prairies (except for numerous foreign groups which have not been assimilated);

The cities of Victoria and Vancouver, and several valleys in British Columbia.

Thus, apart from the Province of Quebec, the British element is to be found everywhere, constituting an appreciable part of the population:

	Per Cent
Maritime Provinces	71
Quebec	15
Ontario	74
The Prairies	50
British Columbia	70

DEMOGRAPHY

In the Maritime Provinces the proportion in New Brunswick is only 62 per cent, and Quebec of course will always disrupt the racial unity of the country.

British supremacy is incontestable in certain zones such as Ontario and British Columbia, and to a lesser degree Nova Scotia and Prince Edward Island. Once French rule had been eliminated, the conquerors were able to colonize the country without hindrance. They alone peopled these immense territories, until the competition of mixed immigration sprang up in the West, which mitigated, or at least deferred their victory. The only region where their offensive has completely failed is the Province of Quebec, where it encountered a block on which it could make no impression.

The British element, according to the census of 1931, represents 52 per cent of the population of Canada, and 11 per cent were actually born in Great Britain. The following table shows that ever since 1871 their proportion has been declining:

Year	British Canadians Total	Per Cent
1871	2,110,502	60
1881	2,548,514	58
1901	3,063,195	57
1911	3,896,985	54
1921	4,868,738	55
1931	5,381,071	51

Their real progress has been substantial because they have drawn their strength from two sources, births and immigration. As opposed to this, however, they have had to compete on two different fronts, against the French Canadian birth-rate and against foreign immigration. As a result the proportion has been falling behind fairly steadily, and, as the years pass, Canada must tend to become less British.

Statistically exact as they are, the proportions quoted above give a false impression, for they do not disclose how powerful a thing the British influence is. This influence is not wholly a matter of the racial composition of the population. The West has been developed, though not exactly peopled, by a ruling class of Scottish and English, who migrated there from the mother country or from the Eastern Provinces. One meets them everywhere, in Winnipeg as in Montreal—maintaining a tradition which is effectively British in a country which otherwise seems more American. Many of these leaders hail from the Maritime Provinces, a fact which is usually not sufficiently emphasized. History records a similar trend in the United States, where the spirit of New England lives again transplanted to the governing class of fifty cities in the West and on the Pacific coast.

§ 2

Examined closely, the sense of the term British is elusive, for today it stands only for political allegiance. Racially and socially it can be broken up into different elements. Having presented the British front—in reality that of the English language—let us now consider in turn the position of the English, Scottish and Irish elements in Canada.

The English, according to official statistics, constitute half the British groups: 2,741,419 out of 5,381,071. They are 26 per cent of the whole population. We find them especially strong in Ontario (where they amount to 52 per cent of the English-speaking people), in the southwest of the Province of Quebec (54 per cent), and in British Columbia (55 per cent). So far as it is possible to ascertain their occupations, one gathers that they are principally civil servants, soldiers or the sons of soldiers, Anglican rectors, wealthy farmers, etc. In a word they form a middle class with a tinge of conservatism, tradition, ritual, and good form. Recently, however, there has been an important change, for immigration seems to be bringing a different type over from England, especially to the West; people of advanced ideas holding the intellectual and political views of the English Labour party. In contrast to these newcomers the Canadians look very conservative! The

English population, of every kind and class, seems to resent the French Canadians with a hostility which is instinctive and congenital. Nothing can be done about it. There is a total lack of understanding, or even of a desire to understand. From this arises the perpetual opposition between the two provinces of Quebec and Ontario.

The Scots are much less numerous, amounting to only 1,346,350 inhabitants, or 25 per cent of the British group, and 13 per cent of the total population. One meets them principally in the Lower Provinces and in the West:

Region	Per Cent of the English-Speaking Population
Prince Edward Island	44
Nova Scotia	36
Manitoba	31
British Columbia	27

They are numerous in Montreal, whereas Toronto is more Anglo-Irish in character. In the Northwest and the Yukon one often finds them among the prospectors. In the township of Glengarry in Eastern Ontario until quite recently the population was so Scottish that Gaelic was often spoken. The characteristics of the Scots are well known: great workers in contrast to the English who sometimes have a reputation for indolence; pro-verbially economical to the point of meanness, while

93

the English are inclined to be spendthrifts; marvellous business men; and, finally, democratic in temperament, in contrast to the hierarchic spirit which never fails the Englishman, be he ever so far to the Left.

The Scots have played an outstanding part in the development of Canada. To the task they brought a serious belief in democracy inspired by reform. This spirit has permeated education. They form the solid backbone of the banking profession, where they stand out as notable personalities with considerable influence. Many of the bankers, as we have already said, come from the Maritime Provinces. In the Montreal telephone directory, the Macs fill six pages. Tear them out, and Montreal is no longer a financial capital, but simply an immense French village with a little English garrison! The Scots do not mix much with the other British elements, but, on the other hand, are on quite friendly terms with the French Canadians. Mixed marriages, which are fairly frequent, often produce people called McDonald or Forbes, who, paradoxically, are French in everything except name! This Scottish tinge explains many things in Canada. A Canadian once summed up the three outstanding characteristics of his country as the climate, the Northland, and the mark of the Scot!

Finally come the Irish, who number 1,230,808, or 23 per cent of the English-speaking group, and 12 per cent of the total population. Apart from the fact that they usually live in the big cities, one cannot say that they are concentrated in any particular district. They can be subdivided into two fundamental groups, according to whether they are Irish Catholics—the real thing! —or Irish Protestants from Ulster. The latter make up the fanatical Protestant element, and are consistently behind the anti-Catholic and anti-French movement in Ontario, where the Orangemen present a replica of the Ku Klux Klan, or a sort of Protestant Tammany. The Irish Catholics, alas, are not much better disposed towards the French Canadians; though they both are Catholics, they speak different languages and are jealous of each other. We thus have a traditional rivalry between two minorities, both of whom are relegated by the English to a lower level, and they detest each other all the more on this account.

A comparison of the census returns, of the English-speaking population taken over a period of 50 years, shows that since 1871 the English have increased from 33 per cent to about 60 per cent of the total, the Scots have maintained their position around 25 per cent, and the Irish have fallen from 41 per cent to 23 per cent. Such statistics suggest that the Irish group is attracting fewer recruits, or is becoming less alive to its own individuality than are the other two. This observation is significant when one recalls the distinct role played by each race in the Canadian community.

The Irish represent—or did in the past—a demagogic ferment of excitement and discord, but also of personality. They provided the agitators and the leaders. The Scots on the contrary are factors of cohesion and bring an essential feeling of solidity which is valuable. As for the English, less gifted according to general opinion, and to tell the truth not very popular, they constitute the social bulwark on which rests the British tradition. In this respect one sees in them what the French Canadians have never been, a ruling class, collectively organized for the direction of the country and at heart always mindful that they are the conquering race. The French in Canada often give the impression of being superior to the others owing to their individual talents, but, as a group, one must admit without hesitation that the English occupy the higher level.

§ 3

Let us now try to ascertain the conditions that have led to the maintenance and development of this powerful British element. They are obliged to defend themselves biologically against the French who are liable to overrun them like tropical vegetation. Socially they must be on their guard against American absorption, which is tending to substitute the very different ideal of a continental North America in place of a British North America. Such problems bring into question the survival of the British as a distinct entity. This brings us to study, in relation to the British Canadians, the same factors we examined earlier in connection with the French. For our purpose we must consider their religion, language, birth-rate, and attitude towards life itself.

The following analysis, made in 1931, shows little change since 1871 in the proportions of the total population claimed by the various religions:

	1931	*Per Cent*
Protestants	5,655,000	55
Catholics	4,285,000	41
Others	436,000	4
		100

If we consider the English-speaking groups separately we find:

	1931	*Per Cent*
Protestants	4,626,369	86
Catholics	691,459	13
Others	63,243	1
		100

Thus 81 per cent of the Protestant element is British. The French Canadians account for only 1.3 per cent of the Protestants, but they represent 66 per cent of the Catholics, in contrast to the British 16 per cent. In a

97

general way one may say that the English Canadians are Protestants, and the French Canadians are Catholics, always bearing in mind, of course, that the English-speaking Catholic minority is by no means negligible, whereas there is no French Protestant minority at all.

But the Protestant churches, as everyone knows, differ radically one from another, so much so that it is necessary to consider them individually: The United Church has 2,017,375 members, making 35 per cent of the total Protestant population; the Anglicans number 1,635,615 members, which is another 29 per cent; Presbyterians add 15 per cent and Baptists 7 per cent, so that these four denominations together represent 85 per cent of the Protestants in the country. The Methodists do not appear in the list, as they were included in the United Church, where they make up about two-thirds of the total. The United Church is a fairly recent attempt at amalgamating some groups of the Protestant denominations. Half the Presbyterians, however, refused to consent to this fusion, and so did the Anglicans and the Baptists. Protestant unity is thus anything but an accomplished fact, which is not surprising since each of these churches corresponds to a certain social strata. The Anglicans are recruited in a somewhat aristocratic way, and naturally are bound up with honours and influence. The Methodists, absorbed into the United Church but not yet digested, represent the middle class, bordering at once on mediocrity on the Left and on wealth on the Right. The Baptists are small-town folk —better not join their ranks if one is a snob.

The appeal of the different denominations is not only a matter of class, but also of national origin. Of the English 41 per cent are Anglicans and 31 per cent United Church, mostly previously Methodists. Of the Scots, 34 per cent are Presbyterians, to whom must be added the greater part of the Presbyterian section of the United Church. As for the Irish, 31 per cent—the real Irish—are Catholics, 32 per cent belong to the United Church, and 17 per cent are Anglicans.

The *Daily Colonist* of Victoria made a suggestive inquiry in its issue of August 25th, 1935, which disclosed that Smiths were either Anglican or Methodist, while the Macs were Presbyterian to a man. In a list of 700 Presbyterian ministers, there were only three Smiths, while out of 875 Anglican parsons and bishops one found eight times as many, 25, to be exact. In 1925 the Methodist preachers who bore this name numbered 36, and in 1935 the United Church contained 52. As for the Macs, they filled two columns of the Presbyterian Year Book, and numbered 120. About 25 per cent of the Presbyterian pastors were Macs. There were four Presbyterian Macs for one Anglican Mac, but there were only two Presbyterian Joneses against 11 Anglican Joneses.

Judging from this, the two currents, English and Scots, have remained relatively distinct. The Presbyterians are definitely in the majority in the Maritime Provinces which are largely peopled by Scots; more Anglicans in Ontario and British Columbia where there are more English; and more members of the United Church in the prairies, where the mixed population includes both English and Scots.

How far can we consider Protestantism as an instrument working to perpetuate the British influence in Canada? To tell the truth, it is a two-edged sword. No doubt there is a general Protestant feeling which is authentically Anglo-Saxon, and inseparable from the English language. In Anglo-French relations, to be Protestant means to be English! Yet, in another sphere, it may play a different role, acting against British influence and favouring Americanization.

Here the distinctions already noted between the various denominations hold good as well; in fact we could easily classify the churches according to their British or American inspiration. In the first rank, and easily in the lead, Anglicanism constitutes a first-rate agent for British unity. In the eyes of its congregation it stands as a national church, reuniting millions of English people all over the world under the same symbols of loyalty. The Presbyterian group also turns back to Europe for its spiritual source, which again strengthens the allegiance to the Old Country. But the Methodist and Baptist Churches, on the contrary, are so American in spirit, in organization and in tradition, that they submit to the continental attraction of the U.S.A. without mental reservations. Even when they wish to be national like the United Church, they are more attached to the religious family of the New World than to that of the Old.

The English language, like the Protestant religion, is also a two-edged weapon. In Canada it is spoken by the British element, and, in fact, by everyone. In this respect it is national, and there is no prospect of its ever being replaced by French. It is thus an instrument of British influence, as is proved by the passionate resistance to the teaching of French everywhere outside the Province of Quebec. Yet English is the tongue common to all the inhabitants of North America, so in this sense it ceases to be just British. It is English if you will, but it would be more accurate to label the North American accent as simply American. In Canada people do not speak in exactly the same way as they do in the United States, but it usually takes a keen ear to detect the difference, which is further proof of the unity of the North American family.

We can thus conclude that the English language is a factor of Canadian political unity, not only with regard to the French who are obliged to learn it, but also with regard to the cosmopolitan immigrants who cannot be assimilated until they have adopted it. When English Canadians protest against the tolerance shown towards the languages of the minorities, they show that they realize what is required to consolidate the Canadian personality under the British aegis. Their indignation at the idea that another language besides English should be spoken in Canada arises assuredly from the well-known Anglo-Saxon laziness when it comes to learning foreign languages. Actually 96 per cent of the Canadians of British origin speak only English! Even the leaders of the political parties, who should in their own interests be able to get into direct contact with the electorate in Quebec, can usually only stammer out the ordinary courtesies, and when absolutely necessary, manage a few words of comic French. But it is *naïveté* even more than laziness.

"How can one be Persian?" as the Parisians of the eighteenth century naïvely asked. Voltaire, in *L'Ingenu*, railed against exactly this state of mind, which after all is common to most peoples. The Abbé St. Yves asked the Ingenu which of the three languages he liked best, Huron, English, or French. "Huron, without a doubt," replied the Ingenu. "Not really!" cried Mademoiselle de Kerkabon. "I always thought that French was the finest language after Low Breton." They then fell to discussing the multiplicity of languages in use, and decided that, had it not been for the Tower of Babel incident, French would have been spoken all over the world.

In Canada the English language has gained the day, but its use does not help the English cause. Through it Americanism is insinuating itself everywhere without let or hindrance. The radio, the press, the theatre, and the "talkies" all diffuse American conceptions just as the wind scatters seeds. Certain parts of the Quebec countryside, where they speak almost nothing but French, are fairly immune, but the English Canadian is absolutely defenceless. The only resistance he can offer against this insidious assimilation is to become excessively British, and so try to emphasize the difference between Canada and the United States.

We must now study the statistics of births and deaths, as we did in the case of the French Canadians. This is the weak point in the British armour. The death-rate in the English provinces is low, no doubt, as in 1934 it amounted to only 9.9 per 1000 in Ontario and 8.8 in British Columbia, but the rate in the Province of Quebec had also fallen to 10.6. It is in the domain of infant mortality that the English maintain their obvious advantage, having only 57 deaths per 1000 births in Ontario and 43 in British Columbia, against 97 in Quebec. (The latter figure was still as high as 127 between 1926 and 1930.) The English birth-rate is showing serious signs of weakness, however. It amounts to 17.5 per 1000 in Ontario and 13.5 in British Columbia, whereas in French Quebec it still remains 25.3 and would be even higher, as we have already noted, if the figures did not include the province's English counties. Thus the contrast between the French and English-speaking districts is complete. This is especially evident when we compare Quebec with those provinces which are socially the most Americanized, such as, for example, British Columbia.

English Canadians, influenced by public opinion in both England and the United States, consider it scandalous for a country to have a high death-rate coincident with a high birth-rate. The aim should be to bring both rates down simultaneously. Malthus is largely responsible for British ideas on this subject: There are too many people in the world, and therefore it is not a duty to give birth to many children. Quality counts above all, and raising the standard of living means raising the standard of morality. In this respect the attitude of the Protestant churches goes directly counter to the doctrines laid down by the French Catholic priests. As a result there is complete disparity in the rhythm of reproduction of the two races. We need only recall that the survival rate in Quebec is 14.7 per 1000, as against only 4.7 in British Columbia. If the French and English Canadians were to embark upon a biological duel the latter would be sure to lose.

In such a contest the antagonism would be not so much between the reproductive capacities, as between the two different ways of looking at life. According to the ethics of French Canadian Catholicism, the individual is obliged to live within a social framework, encompassed by a series of rites which punctuate the passage of the days and years. He submits to the effective direction of a spiritual hierarchy, which extols to the faithful the beauty of sacrifice, the value of discipline, and the virtue of the family. English Canadian Protestantism, on the other hand, puts the accent on man's moral responsibility to his own conscience, with no need for intervention on the part of a sacramental priesthood. In their eyes the development of a material civilization is, in fact if not in doctrine, a form of moral dignity. When the Catholic ideal of renunciation is set aside in this way, the door is open wide to Americanism, which teaches that material progress prevails over spiritual preoccupations.

Between these two perils of Catholicism and Americanism can we still visualize a Canada, tinged with British colour and preserving her integrity? No doubt she will succeed best in her effort to resist Americanism by relying upon Anglicanism, as it furnishes a bulwark, at once moral, aesthetic and social, against American vulgarity. Would such a course not run the risk of tempting her towards Catholic ritual, and thus forfeiting something essentially British? Have no fear. The Anglican looks down from a height upon these French people with their allegiance to Rome, and deems them socially inferior. Because of this resistance to the temptation of neighbours on two fronts, it is possible to conceive of a truly Canadian attitude, with a British background.

CHAPTER VI

IMMIGRATION AND EMIGRATION

THE FUTURE OF THE CANADIAN POPULATION

§ I

IMMIGRATION has played a leading part in the peopling of the American continent, for the whole of the white population has been brought in from outside. Though this vast human displacement has been going on for five centuries, it reached its maximum proportions only during the last hundred years. It should rank among the great feats of history, even surpassing in scope the barbarian invasions of Europe, since it has brought into being a new section of our race, and the one which is capable of becoming, if not the most numerous, at least the richest and most influential.

The North American peoples in so far as they are white, and that is the vast majority, come of ancient stock that went forth from this very old continent of Europe. Yet collectively they have acquired a new personality, arising from the adaptation of old blood to natural surroundings that are much younger, and also from the mingling together of breeds that are dissimilar and scarcely contemporary. The very atmosphere they breathe imparts in them a freshness and originality —in short, turns them into Americans. This applies to Canada quite as much as to the United States.

Historically, the peopling of the United States took place in three successive waves or tides: the first, up to their independence, furnished a stock that was mainly British; the second, in the middle of the nineteenth century, added to this initial foundation a complement of Germans, Irish, and Scandinavians, which has left an indelible mark; the third, from about 1880 up to the Great War, poured in a wave of Slavs and Mediterraneans, which taxed to the utmost the country's hitherto uncontested power of assimilation.

The evolution of Canada presents a parallel to the American example, but with a lag in time, as if the prestige of her great neighbour had irresistibly induced her to follow on after an interval. One distinguishes three phases in the peopling of Canada: the first, from its origins to the end of the nineteenth century; the second, covering the first fourteen years of the twentieth century; and the third, which commenced after the war period and terminated with the world crisis of 1929.

The French must be regarded as the oldest element in the initial formation of the Canadian people, since their earliest colonists left Europe over 250 years ago. When their descendants today lay claim to the un- qualified term Canadian, they are fully within their rights. The English Canadians, by comparison, are new- comers, whether they be the descendants of the Eng- lish immigrants in the eighteenth century of the United Empire Loyalists, or of the colonization which, at the beginning of the nineteenth century, populated Ontario with English. The sources of French immigration dried up completely after 1763.

In the second half of the nineteenth century, immi- gration into Canada was reduced to a mere trickle, amounting, from 1881 to 1902, to 1,322,000, or only 60,000 people a year. The reason was that the Canadian West, though then being organized, was still not equipped to receive immigrants. Also the era of falling prices which began to spread all over the world in 1873, and continued till about 1895, was producing to the full its depressing effects. Canada was more depressed by this stagnation than immigration statistics indicate, because a large proportion of her immigrants in this period did not remain. Until the turning point at the end of the nineteenth century, immediately preceding the opening up of the West, the relative position of the French and Anglo-Saxon elements remained almost un- broken. The 1,322,000 immigrants cited earlier comprised 84 per cent of Americans and British, and only 16 per cent of foreigners.

The great period of Canadian immigration took place at the beginning of the present century, or, to be exact, from 1903 to 1914. The causes of this sudden expansion are easily traced. In the first place there was the appeal of the West, which was being opened up to colonization. The construction of the Canadian Pacific Railway, which had been finished since 1886, was beginning to bear fruit, and after 1904 the construction of two more transcontinental railways, the Grand Trunk Pacific and the Canadian Northern, added fresh incentive. Meanwhile the Liberal Government, which had come into power in 1896, under the premiership of Laurier, embarked on a vigorous immigration policy. He was determined that Canada should not be neglected by the strong current of immigration which was moving from Europe overseas to America. At the same time he solicited British capital, because the immense regions still lying empty in the West obviously could not be exploited without enormous funds. Such were the immediate causes of this revival of immigration. They would not have been sufficient, however, had there not been a definite rise in the economic temperature of the world, as the result of the reversal in the trend of world prices. We breathed freely again—as I well remember—in the exhilarating atmosphere of a thriving commerce which filled our seaports at high tide.

The volume of immigration swelled at this time to astonishing proportions. The total number of immigrants in the twelve years from 1903 to 1914 rose to 2,677,319, a yearly average of 223,000, instead of 60,000 as in the preceding period. In 1912, 1913, and 1914, the average actually rose to 362,000! During the 1902-11 decade, the Canadian population increased more by immigration than by the survival rate of births over deaths, the two figures being 1,659,000 and 854,000.

At the same time this immigration was changing in character:

Period 1903-14

Origin	Immigrants	Per Cent of Total
British	1,087,283	41
United States	842,109	31
Others	747,927	28
	2,677,319	

In the foreign element, which had never previously reached such figures, were included many Nordics—Germans and Scandinavians, who are somewhat akin to the English Canadians in civilization. An exotic type was introduced by Slavs and Mediterraneans, who appeared for the first time in compact groups. Contrary to what is generally believed, an important proportion of the new arrivals between 1903 and 1914 settled in the East, although the main current, or 54 per cent of the total, was destined for the West:

Region	Per Cent of Total
Maritime Provinces	4
Quebec	15
Ontario	27
Prairie Provinces	42
British Columbia	12
	100

The West immediately acquired a cosmopolitan outlook which it still retains, making it quite different in character from Quebec and Ontario. I visited Winnipeg in 1904, at the moment that this tide of immigration was beginning to sweep in. Nothing will give a better idea of its diversity than the statistics of foreigners who were passing in 1903 through this gateway to the West. Winnipeg had become a veritable centre of distribution for the new colonists: [1]

English	20,224
Canadians from the East	16,514
Americans	12,698
Ruthenians	9,514
Germans	7,852
Scottish	7,536
Norwegians	4,363

[1] Figures given by the Commissioner of Immigration at Winnipeg.

Swedes	3,877
Canadians returning from the U.S.A.	3,338
Italians	2,975
Irish	2,521
French	1,156
Hungarians	1,047
Russians	732
Poles	725
Icelanders	692
Hebrews	605
Finlanders	556
Belgians	493
Danes	481
Dutch	381
Bohemians	322
Austrians	297
Galicians	256
Swiss	156
Roumanians	129
Slovaks	99
Greeks	77
Armenians	13
Australians	8
Bulgarians	5
Arabs	4
Brazilians	2

The war naturally brought this influx to an end. Actually the five years from 1915 to 1919 show no more than 344,246 entrants, or a yearly average of only 68,848. Furthermore, three-fifths of them came from the United States, which reduces the number from continental Europe to practically nothing. But with the return of peace a fairly important revival took place, continuing until 1932 when it was stopped in its turn by the world crisis. During the fifteen years from 1920 to 1934, the number of immigrants was 1,523,842, or a yearly average of 102,000, and made up as follows:

Origin	Immigrants	Per Cent of Total
British	634,000	42
American	336,000	22
Cosmopolitan	554,000	36

In 1929, the last year of American prosperity, 167,723 new citizens came into Canada. This immigration was subdivided into racial origins as follows:

Origin	Immigrants	Per Cent of Total
British	75,581	45
Continental European	91,094	54
Non-European	1,047	1

About half the Europeans came from the west and north, the remainder being Slavs, Levantines, and Mediterraneans. Owing to the depression, the Canadian Government is making no efforts to attract immigration for the time being. It has suspended the activities of its immigration offices in the United States, has reduced them in England, and is refusing permission for foreigners to enter the country.

Exotic immigration, i.e., other than the white race, must be considered separately as special conditions arise. The American coast of the Pacific Ocean exerts a magnetic attraction over the yellow race. Owing to their unlimited capacity for work and their low standard of living, they succeed there; and, without doubt, were they allowed to compete freely, they would eventually dominate the western slope of the Rocky Mountains. This tide has been stemmed, however, by regulations supported by military force, so that today there are very few Asiatics on these shores, and the problem is merely a local one. It would be an illusion to think that any real solution has been reached, however, for the pressure of the population of the one continent upon the other still continues.

In 1931 there were in Canada, chiefly in British Columbia, 46,519 Chinese. The Chinese Immigration Act of 1923, following a series of defensive laws passed at intervals since 1885, controls, in fact makes impossible, any further immigration. As for the Japanese, they number 23,342, and, in contrast to the Chinese, have settled with their families. They are also almost all in British Columbia. But according to the Gentlemen's Agreement of 1907 the Tokio Government regulates the issue of passports. This has become so restricted that practically no Japanese have been admitted since 1929. The immigration of Hindus from India into British Columbia, though fairly heavy in 1907 and 1908, has latterly been reduced almost to nothing by appropriate measures. From the narrow point of view of officialdom, the barrier has proved effective, but the problem extends beyond simple frontier regulations, and fundamentally still remains to be reckoned with. We shall return to it later when we discuss the racial security of the country.

§ 2

Let us now analyse the racial composition of the Canadian people, as presented by the excellent statistics of the 1931 census.

Origin	Inhabitants	Per Cent of Total
British	5,381,071	52
French	2,927,990	28
Continental European	1,825,252	17
Others	242,473	3
	10,376,786	100

Together the first two groups form the basis of the population, of which they constitute 80 per cent. Further analysis of the balance shows that 9 per cent of the total population originated in Central, Western, and Northern Europe, 1 per cent in the Mediterranean area, and 7 per cent in Eastern Europe. All except 218,000 inhabitants belong to the white race, and of these 128,890 are Indians and Eskimos.

Certain provinces have a marked demographic tinge.

For example, Ontario is 74 per cent British, Quebec 79 per cent French, the Prairie Provinces 40 per cent cosmopolitan, and British Columbia 7 per cent Asiatic. Although the same cannot be said of most of the Latin American countries south of the Rio Grande, we may conclude that Canada is preponderantly white as distinct from Asiatic and Red Indian, and British and French rather than cosmopolitan. Nevertheless these cosmopolitans, who have come from Europe (apart from France), are numerous, and their assimilation is a very real problem.

The assimilation of every immigrant means a struggle within his very being. The first factor is historical: he must break the ties which still bind him to his native land. The second is geographic: he must accustom himself to the soil and the climate. The third is social: he must adapt himself to a new environment. When we speak of Canadian assimilation, however, this third factor is not clearly defined, for the environment will be French in Quebec, and English or even American everywhere else. Thus the alternatives are assimilation to the French or to the Anglo-Saxon type. The French group, as we have shown, can absorb individuals, but in the end this assimilation of foreigners works in favour of Anglo-Saxon culture and the English language.

Assimilation is rapid, almost immediate, for British

and Americans, easy for Germans and Scandinavians, but slow for Ukrainians, Slavs, and Mediterraneans. The latter hold aloof in their own villages, speaking their own language, but in time they learn English and finally fuse into their surroundings. To the Ukrainians and Poles, the West in its featureless immensity recalls their native land. The Catholic Church, in spite of resistance within itself, favours English as being the most convenient means of communication for the faithful in America.

Assimilation does invariably take place, just as it does in the United States and for the same reasons. It is continental in character. The former European becomes North American, but not inevitably British or Anglo-Saxon. A distinction thus arises between different types of citizens. The veritable test of British assimilation is the civic sense, the recognition of social collaboration as a duty, which is so remarkable among well-bred English people. Now the immigrant, more often than not, does not acquire this sense. He gets profit and nothing more out of the community that has received him. It is the pure English stock, carrying out the functions of the aristocracy, which maintains the tradition of civic duty. Thus the quality of the community may not be improved by the infusion of this new blood, but the Anglo-Saxon group benefits nevertheless, as English is eventually imposed as the prevailing tongue.

These different elements and their respective reactions constitute a clearly defined problem. The French Canadians, being unable to add to their numbers by either immigration or assimilation, are reduced to depending on their birth-rate, while immigration and assimilation continue to reinforce the English-speaking section. This brings us to the conclusion that although immigration is not the principal factor in peopling the country, it acts as a regulator and directly affects the composition of the population. When immigration ceases or even declines the percentage of French Canadians rises; when it revives, this percentage diminishes, to the benefit of the Anglo-Saxon element.

This equilibrium is liable to be further modified by another factor, namely emigration. This brings us back to the question of the axis which serves as the *leitmotiv* of this book. The east-west current brings immigration over from Europe, and directs it westwards across the continent towards the prairies and British Columbia. But the north-south current is always present, silently, anonymously, persistently, irresistibly, and fatally, turning men's minds towards the United States.

At times the movement is in the other direction, as for example at the beginning of the present century, when the American farmers were ready to exchange their cultivated lands for virgin soil in the Canadian West. Basically, however, the attraction is towards the South, as if the great mass of the American nation were blindly obtruding its presence in fulfilment of the universal law of gravitation. The reasons are simple enough. In times of prosperity, or even when there is not an acute depression, American prestige shines like a sun. In the neighbouring country, which is more modest and less brilliantly lit up, people feel that in this vast neighbouring theatre there must be more chances of success, and so there are. The Canadians who are tempted to leave their own country belong to all classes and all races. Among them are workmen looking for employment at higher wages, like the French Canadians who emigrated in hundreds of thousands into New England; there are engineers, professors, industrialists, and business men of all kinds, ambitious young fellows who find Canada too small—all going forth to make their fortunes more quickly on the other side of the frontier. The atmosphere of the two countries is so much alike that they become assimilated almost immediately.

The great Canadian journalist, Mr. John W. Dafoe, gives the following striking examples of this migration: "An inquiry some years ago showed that 13 per cent of the graduates of Canadian universities were living in the United States. A university in the Maritime

Provinces gave American addresses for 34 per cent of its graduates. Some years ago the entire graduating class in engineering in a Canadian university found within a year occupations in the United States." [1]

These deserters act in perfectly good faith, for, as the two countries are so similar, they do not feel that they are being traitors. There are also the immigrants from Europe, who declare quite frankly that they have every intention of going on farther, and are only stopping in Canada in *transit*. This whole frontier gives the impression of a dam that has not been made properly water-tight, for it cannot retain the population, which keeps draining away. The attraction of far off fields is not sufficient to account for this chronic leakage. Circumstances do exist within the country itself, however, to render it inevitable, i.e., a high birth-rate coinciding with the heavy immigration of the past forty years. As the increment from these two sources cannot be immediately absorbed, part of the old population has been obliged to emigrate.

The loss through this persistent emigration is enormous. The Government Statistics Bureau estimates the amount of this human deficit by the following calculations:

[1] *Canada, an American Nation*, John W. Dafoe, p. 101, Columbia University Press, 1935.

Decade	1901-10	1911-20	1921-30
Total Population at Beginning of Decade	5,371,315	7,206,643	8,787,949
Natural Increase	853,566	1,150,125	1,325,256
Immigration	1,847,651	1,728,921	1,509,136
Total	8,072,532	10,085,689	11,622,341
Actual Population at End of Decade	7,206,643	8,787,949	10,376,786
Loss through Emigration	865,889	1,297,740	1,245,555

The 1911-20 loss also includes the 60,000 Canadian soldiers who died overseas.

The accuracy of this reasoning is proved by the fact that the loss of three and a half million citizens owing to emigration as worked out above for the full thirty year period corresponds approximately to the number of Canadians who have found their way to the United States. The report of the Commissioner of Immigration at Washington for the year 1932 shows that 3,337,-345 Canadians are now living in the United States. The most superficial impression obtained by travelling will confirm that this figure is not exaggerated, for the northern states, bordering on the frontier, seem filled with Canadians, both English and French. Although excellent citizens of their new community, they are still mindful of their country of origin. In several cities one finds in the leading hotels a special floor reserved for the Canadian Club, and in New England the Franco-American element makes its presence felt at every turn and in heavy doses.

The deficit of three million souls—equal almost to one-third of the Canadian population—is a cruel loss. It must definitely be written off as a loss, for although some emigrants do return, the great majority are swallowed up by the American masses. North-south, the trend is irresistible, in spite of occasional eddies moving in the other direction. The Canadian Government is rowing against the current, and is obliged to keep up a continuous political struggle to counteract this natural appeal.

We are now ready to come to certain conclusions with regard to the future of the Canadian population, or at least to make a few comments. In the first place we may say that it is mediocre in volume compared with the United States, or even with England. Thirty years ago people, especially Imperialists, used to say that the day would come when Canada would have a larger population than the mother country! Today this no longer seems possible, and, what is more important, the English realize it. They know that England will continue to be the most important block of white population in the Empire. So Canada will probably remain a community of secondary importance between Britain and the United States, in spite of the enormous size of her territory.

For any rapid increase to take place, immigration must be revived on a large scale. Now in this respect we must realize that the nineteenth century and the period up to the war offered exceptional circumstances. Europe wished to divest herself of her excess population, which the new countries were ready to receive. At the same time the surplus capital which had accumulated in the old countries was being attracted overseas to be invested in opening up virgin territories. In the beginning of the twentieth century, from 1900 to 1914, Canada was developed under this system, according to which Europe dispensed both emigrants and capital.

But today, although the old continent still overflows with people, they are no longer anxious to leave home to make their fortunes abroad. They now have a standard of living which they believe to be guaranteed by the State, and even if they did wish to settle abroad they are not allowed to do so. The new communities close their doors on the slightest pretext, for fear of absorbing undesirables and creating unemployment. It is well known that it is practically impossible to obtain authorization to settle in the United States, and, since 1930-31, the Canadian immigration policy has been equally defensive. No doubt with the return of prosperity, even to a limited degree, the regulations will be eased up and the human current will be allowed to flow once more, but it is not likely that it will ever be so great as in the past.

This hypothesis is interesting, however, owing to its future repercussions not merely on the volume but also on the composition of the Canadian population. Immigration has tended to make Canada less strictly British perhaps, but indirectly more Anglo-Saxon, and relatively less French. If the present policy of shutting out immigration is continued—in 1934 it fell to 13,903—it will have the effect sooner or later of increasing the French percentage, perhaps rather quickly. This will create serious problems, far surpassing cold statistics. What will be the British reaction when the proportion of French Canadians rises above 30 per cent, and, perhaps, passes 35 per cent? Racial minorities are treated benevolently when they are declining, for then they are not dangerous, but they arouse fierce antagonism when they are increasing.

I cannot picture the French Canadians attaining the majority, but if they did the English would never be willing to accept second rank numerically. They would revolt. They might prefer to secede, who knows! This, I repeat, will not happen, but even a trend in this direction is sufficient to arouse a latent hostility, and bring about defensive measures. Would the English group, for example, consider deliberately fostering an artificial type of immigration in order to furnish themselves with recruits? Or would they try to limit, in the scholastic domain, any development likely, in their eyes, to endanger Canadian unity in its British form? The answer raises questions of psychology, of politics, and even of the economic equilibrium of the country.

III

THE ECONOMIC ASPECT

CHAPTER VII

AGRICULTURE

I. THE FRENCH CANADIAN PEASANT

§ 1

CANADA is essentially a country of natural resources, with apparently inexhaustible potentialities in agriculture, forestry, and mining. Her manufacturing industries are developing at the same time, but the country seems to be better adapted to the initial processing of raw materials than to the production of finished products. In 1933 this "primary" production accounted for 53 per cent of the value of the country's total output, the remaining 47 per cent being accounted for by "secondary," or manufacturing production. (In 1929, before the depression, these proportions were respectively 47 per cent and 53 per cent.)

This group of primary products was made up as follows:

	Per Cent of Total Production
Agriculture	28
Mines	10
Electric power	6

	Per Cent of Total Production
Forestry	7
Fisheries and Furs	2
	53

As this distinction between primary and secondary products is becoming more and more difficult to define, the statisticians are obliged to become more flexible and to make their entries under more than one heading. This is necessary because in America more than anywhere else intensively mechanized industrial methods in both theory and practice have penetrated to the heart of agriculture, and are even carried on in the virgin forests. Such contrasts properly belong to the New World, which had been the pioneer in mechanization. More and more one meets manufacturing operations at every stage from raw material production at the one end of the scale, to urban distribution at the other.

In agriculture especially mechanization is now intervening to increase the scope of the cultivator. In the new countries this evolution is rapidly modifying, almost to the point of reversing the established equilibrium between the urban and rural population. Every activity on the part of the farmer now necessitates a corresponding activity from another man in the city.

In Canada the percentage of urban population rose from 32 per cent in 1891 to 54 per cent in 1931, the

provinces with the largest urban population being the
following:

	Urban Population Per Cent
Quebec	63
Ontario	61
British Columbia	57

In contrast to this group, the Maritime and Prairie
Provinces have remained largely rural, although even
here the urban element represents an important minority:

	Per Cent
Maritime Provinces	38
Manitoba	45
Saskatchewan	32
Alberta	38

It is essential to grasp the significance of this urbani-
zation, for although it admits of dangers which seem
obvious to us in Europe, it is normal in the New World,
for it is in keeping with the spirit and methods of our
time.

The agricultural development of Canada extends
over three phases which succeed one another, and yet
coincide. In its early days the country was given up to
fishing, hunting and trapping, which are still continued,
particularly by the French Canadians and the Scots.
Then came the first agricultural establishments, when
part of the population settled along the shores of the

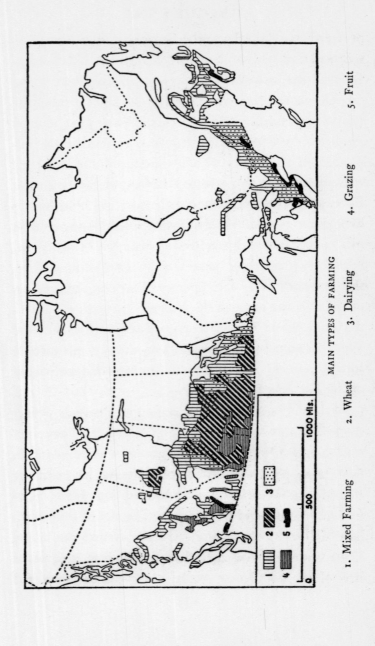

MAIN TYPES OF FARMING

1000 Mls.

500

0

1. Mixed Farming   2. Wheat   3. Dairying   4. Grazing   5. Fruit

St. Lawrence. Thanks to the French, a European peasant tradition was implanted, but with the notable difference that cultivation in a new country had to be carried out on a more extensive scale. During the nineteenth and twentieth centuries the two great natural resources, wood and wheat, were systematically exploited, in conformity with advanced technical methods that were gradually perfected. Lumbering in its various forms put the pioneer into contact with the most highly developed type of industry, and wheat farming with mechanized methods soon became the law of the West. Although these three phases still exist simultaneously, they are not really contemporary. The French Canadian of today is the same as the French Canadian of yesterday, and herein lies his strength; the cultivator of the West has no past but may exist tomorrow, and his whole force lies in the present and the future; but the people of the Far North are eternal.

A classification of the various regions reveals differences which are no less important. First, the East especially is devoted to mixed farming—cereals, cattle, dairy products, fruit and vegetables—which in many ways still belongs to the peasant tradition. Here, however, we are aware of the double influence of the neighbouring forest, and of the American civilization of the great cities. Then, secondly, in the western prairies, as well as in the fruit-growing districts of Niagara and

British Columbia, we find ourselves confronted with the most modern types of farming. Thirdly come those regions which are only now being cleared of the forest. As they combine mixed farming with the spirit of the pioneer rather than that of the peasant, we must classify apart the regions which are still being opened up. This zone includes the *hinterland* of the St. Lawrence in both Quebec and Ontario, and the country fringing the wheat belt in the West, on the edge of the Laurentian Shield. Still farther on begins the endless domain of fishing and trapping.

Each of these different types of production has its own market. The first and third groups sell their goods locally, and as their activities are diversified they have been little affected by the depression. The second, American in character, exports, on the contrary, enormous quantities to the international markets. As its very law of existence is relentless specialization, it must bow beneath the lash of world depressions.

Several social types are linked up with this division of agricultural production. Two in particular stand out clearly, forming the opposite poles: the French Canadian, peasant, pioneer, and superior in the practice of traditional virtues, is bound up with mixed farming, and scarcely interested in exports. The other, whom we shall describe as American, is superior in technique, an agricultural industrialist rather than a farmer. He is devoted to the machine and to the specialization of crops, but is dependent on international consumption. We have purposely over-simplified this classification for the sake of clarity, for there also exist other important intermediary types, such as the Ontario farmer of English and Scottish descent, who is an agriculturist born and bred. He recalls the substantial German peasants of Central Europe and the Danube Basin, and at the same time he is very like the American farmer. There is also the Ukrainian or Polish immigrant who has arrived more recently on the western prairies. He brings with him the oldest peasant tradition of all, and yet he can be Americanized very rapidly once his roots with his fatherland are severed. Finally the Japanese in British Columbia, who toils unremittingly and subsists on a standard of living with which it is impossible to compete. His mere presence is an uneasy reminder that Asia is close at hand.

These different types of humanity, their contacts and combination in a new political community, create a distinct problem. They do not adapt themselves according to the same rhythm, for the American type progresses too quickly for the European peasant who clings persistently to his early traditions. The latter is perhaps the most interesting aspect of the problem, and at times one wonders whether there is really room in North America for the peasant conception.

§ 2

The French Canadian is a peasant. The Americans delight in announcing aggressively that they have no peasants in the United States! Actually they have only agricultural industrialists, who have broken away completely from the patrimony of the old rural civilizations. The term "peasant" no doubt is equivocal, for it suggests a serf attached to the glebe. But in employing it in the French sense which carries no sting, we are tempted to reply that if America did have peasants she would be much better off! The strength and dogged resistance of this type of humanity was shown up clearly by the depression, especially in the New World.

One soon perceives that the real strength of the French Canadian peasant is that he has remained true to his tradition. He is a countryman, in touch with Nature, and attached to the soil whether he be a lumberjack or a farmer. If this race is urbanized to excess, as is happening in the Province of Quebec where the cities are now absorbing 63 per cent of the population, it loses the source of its vitality. Its moral fortress lies in the countryside, in the rural parishes where the priest can still gather his flock around him. There the old Canadian type is still unspoiled by outside influences, but we may well wonder how long it can last. For it to survive we must have the consent of the women and children, and here again we must turn to the *curé*, the essential piece in the system, on whom depends any hope of resistance. But have no illusions, he is definitely on the defensive.

One should distinguish between the arable lands which have given rise to the peasant type, and the forest zones which have necessitated the pioneer. In Eastern Canada the farmer is the *habitant* who tills the soil, the same soil since the early days of the French colonization. It is astonishing to find how narrow is the strip of cultivated land. In the St. Lawrence Valley one is immediately confronted with the Laurentian Mountains on the edge of the Laurentian Shield. From the heights of the Dufferin Terrace at Quebec one can discern, only a few miles away, that blue line which marks the end of human habitation; beyond it rock and forest still wait to be conquered. This is the domain of the pioneer. The immense North Country comes down so close that one can almost touch it with the hand.

The Canadian peasant seems unexpected and paradoxical in the New World. He is the symbol of tradition and stability, following a philosophy of life which is associated with the countryside of France, and quite distinct from that of the United States. One feels his fundamental opposition to Americanism the moment that one comes into contact with him. His qualities as a rural farmer are classic. He is a worker, never shrinking from physical effort; he is thrifty; he is much less of a speculator than the American, and not in such a hurry. His ideal is to live on the land and from the land, to bring up his children on it, to establish them on it, and finally to hand it on to them. That is all. There is a biblical grandeur in such simplicity.

The essential factor is the attachment to the soil. It is this which makes the French Canadian so exceptional in a continent where they buy, sell, and swap farms, like stocks and shares. The American has cut adrift from the anchor which in the past has enabled mankind to survive the storm. The Canadian, on the other hand, holds sacred the wholesome qualities of the earth, and still regards a home on the land as the best security. Like the old-established rural communities he has the capacity of drawing both pleasure and profit from tilling the soil. What M. Mauriac said about the French peasant applies equally well to the Canadian. It requires exceptional anchors to hold on the land that part of humanity which feeds the rest.[1]

There are two definitely opposed conceptions of what man may demand from the land. On the one hand is the type of agriculture with which one can make a living but not grow rich. It is a mode of life, but not a means of making a fortune. This is exactly what the American cannot abide, for he wants to get rich, and

[1] François Mauriac, *La Provence*, p. 36.

get rich quickly. True, he will cultivate the land, often exceedingly well, but he is more preoccupied with buying and selling it, and putting by a visible cash profit which he can mobilize if he wishes to go elsewhere. Above all he neither knows how to wait nor wishes to learn. He has lost the instinct for Time, which is the safeguard of the peasant. The latter, on the contrary, knows that he can obtain a living from the land, but that it is unwise to expect much more. The profit, the benefit, to which he looks forward, does not appear in book-keeping, for the most successful rural balance sheet is not based on two-and-two-make-four. The priest and the family doctor understand these things better than the expert and the social service worker. But how old-fashioned all this is, and how un-American!

In the French districts of the St. Lawrence Valley the average farm consists of a hundred acres, and is run by a peasant proprietor. These farms are all alike, long rectangular bands lying perpendicular to the road, with the house situated at the end. Mixed farming is the rule, producing cereals, milk and butter, chickens, vegetables, and a few fruit trees. It is what the Germans call *natural wirtschaft*. The family lives on the farm which is a complete production unit. They consume much of what is produced and they sell what they can in the neighbouring market, which is often the big town. The farmer himself does the work with the assistance of his wife, his sons, and his daughters, without depending much on hired labour or machinery. He is always in touch with the Church. This system gives satisfactory results. Technically it is inferior to the American, but it is not industry disguised, and can still be called agriculture.

In order to decide whether there is anything here worth saving, we must not look at the matter purely as experts. As is the case in Europe, the peasant does not take his own work into account, at least not all of it, when calculating his costs. He saves in order to establish his children on neighbouring farms, or to round off his own holding. He also borrows, being a man of the New World, but less than the American, for property mortgaged in his eyes is "property owed." In the height of prosperity others earn more than he does, but he weathers hard times better, especially as having inherited his farm he has not paid too much for it. He was jeered at during the boom, but he seemed very wise during the crisis. If prosperity returns he will be laughed at again for not keeping up with the times and the ways of the New World. Who is right? Perhaps the American conception of agriculture will have to be revised one day, and, meanwhile, are they not asking the French Canadian farmer to go too far and too quickly? Like Antheus, the mythological figure, he has to keep touching the soil if he is to remain strong or even to survive.

§ 3

The clearing of new land is still essential. Farms are not subdivided but remain the same size as in the past, partly because of the low productivity of agriculture and partly because it is customary to hand on the property intact to the eldest son. Therefore, in the regions which have already been developed, sooner or later there is not sufficient cultivated land to go round. In spite of a low density per square mile, over-population already exists, so part of the family is forced to migrate. The factory near by, or in the United States, offers an outlet for workmen, and the city awaits those entering liberal professions or commerce. But the traditional career, always open to the man with initiative, is that of the pioneer.

The task of clearing new land is inconceivably hard. The forest is there, and the pioneer must conquer it. First the trees must be felled one by one. If they are saplings it may be possible to cultivate the soil in the following year, but if they are full-grown the stumps will not rot away for seven or eight years, and they cannot be removed until then. Meanwhile the pioneer sells the timber, picks up a job here and there, or works on a neighbouring farm. Often he has to be supported by his relatives.

The French Canadians resent being held up to admiration for their pioneering, and give a cool reception to novels written by foreigners in which this aspect of their national life is described at length. Yet they have a genius for this difficult and magnificent work, which daunts both the English and those who have become Americanized. Scots, Scandinavians and Finns know how to pioneer, but in Canada it is still the descendants of the French, with their simple needs and powers of endurance, who are best able to tackle the job. Such negative qualities are seldom found now in America, where they are more likely to be despised than regarded as virtues.

Around Lake St. John the forest has long since been attacked, and also along the Richelieu River, in the Gaspé Peninsula, at Abitibi and Temiskaming. On the prairies a partially wooded or park-like territory situated north of the wheat belt is being colonized seriously, and so further to the northwest is the Peace River district, which alluring prospectuses recommend as "colonization de luxe." Along the edge of these territories a career is still open to the pioneer as it is in the Northwest near Lake Athabaska, Great Slave Lake, and Peel River.

In Canada there are certain districts which the French

Canadian seemed destined to appropriate. Wherever there are insuperable difficulties, one is sure to find him. On the open prairies where there are no trees to be cleared he is no better than anyone else, but among rocks and forests, where streams babble over the stones —there he is in his element. Even in intermediary zones, half forest and half clearing, he will throw himself heart and soul into a family effort at mixed farming.

In 1935 I visited a farm not far from Edmonton, Alberta, beyond the wheat belt where the country is somewhat wooded. The farmer, a French Canadian who had previously been established at Lake St. John, had bought the land in its virgin state, a single quarter section of 640 acres. He and his two sons had cleared it with machinery. It was not without emotion that I witnessed their first crop of wheat growing in a field where trees had stood only a year before. We no longer have such beginnings in Europe! This farm was much the same as it would have been in Quebec. The family consisted of the farmer himself; his wife, who went to market; their two daughters, who took care of the house but spoke hardly any English; two stalwart sons, one in charge of the animals, and the other in charge of the machinery. They had fifteen machines, a repair shed, and two private motor cars. Then I was taken to see the pigs, the chicken run, and the vegetable garden —but the depression was never even mentioned!

When we reflect on the loss of vitality which the French Canadian race has suffered owing to the exodus into the towns and into the New England cotton mills, we can understand how a new doctrine of colonization could have been developed towards the end of the last century. It was really based on the spirit of national preservation. "Keep our people together in a land where they can maintain their own individuality," was the watchword of the great leader, Father Labelle. The development of Lake St. John and other similar districts was the result. When the Laurier cabinet proposed a new transcontinental railway, the Grand Trunk Pacific, as part of their platform at the 1904 elections, the French in the lower St. Lawrence were interested only in the section which would link Quebec City with Winnipeg by the northern route. They saw, and with reason, a new basis for French expansion, where their people would not be lost to their own country.

Since then the Government of the Province of Quebec has followed this colonization policy, for it reflects a definite conviction on their part. Under its present form, existing parishes are first developed by sending out and financing colonists who complete the work of clearing. New parishes are also opened up. The Government furnishes the social framework by subsidizing the colonists—men, women, and children—who form the initial population. They also take care to provide the priests. The aim always is to colonize, but the essential condition is the establishment of a definite French Canadian group.

The difficult thing about such an enterprise, especially in a country like Canada, is to recruit people who are really going to settle down in good faith. When things are going badly everywhere, they accept their lot, and for want of something better will go to open up arduous country. When prosperity returns, however, they are tempted to leave the forest and migrate to the towns or to the United States. When one thinks of the contrast between this rough life and the material comfort of the American standard of living, what anchor—to borrow Mauriac's expression—can possibly hold them to the land which they are supposed to be bringing within the pale of civilization? It is no use trying to restrain them. Success lies perhaps in getting them to accept frankly a certain conception of life—the one for which the priest has become the champion.

In a letter dated July 8th, 1935, in reply to one from me asking for information, a French Canadian of Quebec, who is closely associated with this fine work of colonization, writes the following significant passage: "These advantages are offered to all who wish to become colonists, and have been accepted by the colonization societies. There are no restrictions with regard to racial origin or religious belief. . . . But I am definitely of the opinion that the French Canadians will be almost the only ones to profit to any extent by this policy. Our roots, which for a generation have been running along the surface, should now penetrate deeply underground. You will understand as well as I do the strength which we shall derive from this. Our parishes, like mushrooms, will spring up everywhere, especially in the northwest of Quebec, beyond the Laurentian Mountains. The country is rough, but so is our race. The struggle will be hard, but once again Nature will be conquered by our people. I look forward to a day when they will overflow naturally into Northern Ontario, where already they have made a foothold. They will first surround with their parishes the little mining towns, which are bound to multiply in this vast region, which is so rich in mineral wealth.

"Elisée Reclus loved Canada, and Canada returned his love in full measure. Reclus was an intimate friend of Mgr. Labelle, our colonizing *curé*, who towards the end of last century did such marvellous work in the inhospitable Laurentian country. Reclus once wrote to him more or less to this effect: 'My Dear Old Labelle: Send your colonists towards the north, far from the American frontiers. Send them where the winters are long and the climate rigorous, where families are numerous and the race is strong.' The dream of these two men is now being realized, and on what a scale! I should like to be still in this world twenty-five years hence, for I believe that by that time we shall have made astounding progress."

We have all heard the much-quoted rejoinder of the Commissioner of National Defence who, when the German army threatened his town in 1870 ordered the commander of a battalion of militia to hold up their advance. "What if they arrive in overwhelming numbers?" he was asked. "Fight until you are all killed," was his light-hearted reply.

Seated at my work table, surrounded not by trees which must be felled, but with documents which must be read, I sometimes feel like such an arm-chair general when I encourage our Canadian friends to go into the forest and conquer it. And yet, if their race is to survive, it will be, as Elisée Reclus has said, by accepting a stern rule of life and not by emulating the American standard of comfort, which they describe with such pride when they come over to France. In the United States they firmly believe that the happiness and degree of civilization of a people is measured by its standard of living. Although this doctrine does not reject work, effort, or enterprise, on the other hand it does condemn all sense of restraint, economy and voluntary sacrifice. Now up to the present the French Canadians owe their progress essentially to a different and almost contrary inspiration.

The problem to consider is whether Canada, situated

so close to the United States with its prodigious standard of living, can retain her peasants. In order to resist this attraction which is already draining away her people, should she not take the initiative herself and become, to a certain extent, Americanized? Are not her peasant folk, in the atmosphere of North America, something of an anachronism?

The agricultural crisis presents yet another problem. Can America, with an urban system which is out of touch with its rural foundation, live indefinitely without peasants? Will she not be obliged to accept an agricultural policy, which, though adapted, of course, to her new conditions, is yet definitely linked up with peasant traditions? The post-war depression clearly showed that the agricultural industrialist of the strictly American type could not weather an economic blizzard with any real resistance. It is to the agricultural industrialist, as he is found in Canada, that we propose to devote our next chapter.

CHAPTER VIII

AGRICULTURE

2. THE WESTERN WHEAT GROWER

§ 1

A VIVID contrast exists between the French Canadian peasant and the wheat producer of the West; it is a contrast of farming technique, of attitude towards life, and even of degree of civilization.

Economically wheat is of vital importance to Canada, especially in its international aspect. To celebrate the coronation of Edward VII, at the time when the prairies were first beginning to be colonized, the Canadians erected in London on the route of the procession a triumphal arch made of sheaves of wheat. Since then Canada has become the greatest wheat exporting country in the world, supplying as much as 48.6 per cent of international requirements in 1925-26. During the prosperous post-war years, 30 per cent of Canada's exports consisted of wheat, and in 1934 it still accounted for 20 per cent, or 23 per cent if flour is included. This expansion is comparatively recent, for it goes back only to the first years of the present century. It is linked up with the growth of the three western provinces of Manitoba, Saskatchewan, and Alberta. A new country has thus arisen beyond the Great Lakes, entirely different in tradition from the historical region of the St. Lawrence. The old opposition between Upper and Lower Canada, between Ontario and Quebec, still exists, but it is overshadowed today by the contrast between the atmosphere of the East and of the West. This has completely altered the equilibrium of the country.

The great progress made during the war brought Canada's wheat area up to twenty-five million acres. Over nine-tenths of this area is in the three Prairie Provinces, forming a triangle: Winnipeg, Calgary, Edmonton. The base of the triangle from Winnipeg to Calgary is about 625 miles. This triangle is bounded on the south by a stretch of prairie grassland, and on the north by a sparsely wooded region which extends as far as the Laurentian Shield, where habitation ceases, and the density of the population falls to one person per square mile! In conformity with the trend towards the west, which is also taking place in the United States, Manitoba, as a producer of cereals, has gradually fallen behind the other two provinces. Winnipeg is still incontestably the economic capital of the western prairies, but Regina is destined to be the geographical centre of the wheat belt.

How vividly one recalls this country: an immense

plain, almost devoid of trees, absolutely flat, as wide as the ocean, rising at times in undulations like a powerful ground swell. The sky is unbelievably clear, and the air as exhilarating as at sea; the very spaciousness fills one with an elementary enthusiasm. The delicate colours of the landscape fade at the horizon into luminous tints of yellow or mauve; the few rivers are torpid or muddy. At the end of this apparently endless region the Rockies rise like a barrier, pink at sunrise and blue in the evening and in the twilight. In this borderland the soil is a magnificent ochre, slashed by rapid watercourses with steep banks. The impression is African rather than Nordic, though the heart of the wheat country suggests Eastern Europe, as M. Paul Morand has remarked in describing his journey across the Northwest: "The ears of wheat undulated as in Samson and Delilah, two Hungaries and four Roumanias placed end to end." [1]

Why should this region be devoted almost exclusively to wheat? Its predominance is obviously due to the formation of the plain, which stretches away unbroken as if the whole country were one immense field. It is therefore exceptionally suitable to the use of machinery. The nature of the soil, rich in silt, lends itself, and so does the climate, which stores up moisture under the snow, and then in summer distributes all the sun-

[1] Paul Morand, *Rien que la Terre*, p. 17.

light required even quite far north, thus forming a curious northern bulge in the isotherms. No country could be better adapted to the cultivation of cereals.

In 1934 Canada came fifth among the wheat-producing countries of the world, after Russia, the United States, India, and France, with 275 million bushels, or 8 per cent of the world total of 3390 million bushels. The three prairie provinces of the West account for 95 per cent of this figure (Manitoba 13 per cent, Saskatchewan 41 per cent, and Alberta 41 per cent). Canada has attained this important position in our day, for the present development had scarcely begun when I visited North America for the first time in 1898. The following table shows how her production was accelerated by the high prices paid during and after the war. The peak was reached in the record year of 1928, only to fall again during the depression of 1934 and 1935:

Year	Wheat Output
1900	47 million bushels
1911	227 " "
1915	392 " "
1928	566 " "
1934-35	275 " "

In view of her acreage, Canada's production is mediocre, but so far as exports are concerned she holds a leading place. The United States, although a great exporter of wheat in the past, now plays a minor part, as is to be expected considering there are 130 million consumers within the country. Canada, on the other hand, having a population of only 10 million, obviously cannot absorb all the wheat she produces, so her exports now amount to about two-thirds of her harvest:

	Per Cent
1900	31
1917-18	72
1925-26	78
1934-35	59
1935-36	75

Under such conditions it is not surprising that Canada should have become the principal source of wheat for the international market, although prior to 1914 the world relied on other countries:

Country	Per Cent of International Requirements before 1914
Russia	24
United States	16
Danube Countries	16
Canada	14

During the war, when there were no shipments from Russia and the Danube Basin, an undreamed-of opportunity opened up for non-European countries such as the United States, Argentina, Australia, and, above all, Canada, and by 1917-18 the latter was supplying 46 per cent of the world's exports. Her predominance continued for some time after the war. From 1924 to

1929 Canada furnished an average of 39 per cent of international exports, and even 48 per cent in 1925-26, at which time the United States supplied 22 per cent, Argentina 19 per cent, and Australia 12 per cent.

The Canadians may have believed that this exceptional position had been acquired permanently, but this was hardly likely. The depression which recently settled on their wheat export trade was in reality very largely the liquidation of the abnormal conditions created by the war. A revival of European production and even exportation was inevitable. Each country, whether well adapted to it or not, began to produce wheat again and even more than before. In 1934 Germany produced 166 million bushels, and Italy 232 million, while Russia, Roumania, Algeria, and even France, exported it. Insurmountable barriers were raised to defend their national production from foreign competition, even by countries depending upon imports. Their war experiences led them to further their nationalist aims by a battery of infinitely diverse and most effective customs tariffs, quotas, licences, import monopolies, preferential treaties, control and depreciation (more or less voluntary) of currencies, price-fixings, premiums, even including domestic regulation of flour milling. The countries which exported the most were naturally the most affected, and in the case of Canada this was the principal cause of her difficulties. The competition of other exporters, who were better placed in some respects, exaggerated the crisis. In 1934 the Argentine captured from her the first place in the international market, by supplying 35 per cent of the world's export trade, while Canada followed with 32 per cent.

There are, however, other aspects of the wheat crisis which may be simply circumstantial, but which, on the contrary, may be destined to last. For example, the *per capita* consumption of bread has declined considerably during the past generation, in France from 492 lbs. in 1909-14 to 418 in 1929-34, and in England from 363 lbs. to 297; it would be imprudent to count on a reversal of this tendency. In addition, Europe has traditionally been a large importer of wheat, and has paid for it by her exports of manufactured goods. How can she reasonably continue now that the world's markets are slipping away from her?

Under such circumstances Canada's wheat exports naturally melted away, falling in 1934 to less than a third of what they were in 1928—from $407,564,561 to $118,969,445. Meanwhile the unsold stocks, which are now in process of rapid liquidation, were accumulating, until they reached 193 million bushels in 1935. England absorbs about 70 per cent of the Canadian wheat exports, for with her preferential tariff, she accords them a privileged market. But there still remains 30 per cent to be disposed of on the international market, in open competition and against a certain amount of nationalistic ill-will which may last and even become aggravated instead of melting away in the sunshine of returning prosperity. From this point of view, Europe, with her bitter political rivalries, does not present a very engaging prospect, and although the Far East has begun to import wheat, its progress is bound to be slow. For Canada the question is not and cannot be exclusively imperial, for to her the international market is essential. As we have already emphasized, she cannot hope to live an independent life of her own. If she is not to be absorbed into the North American mass as Pan-Americanism would suggest, she must accept a certain amount of internationalism.

Thus the Canadian wheat problem must be approached from an international angle. We must guard against generalizing on the basis of events which are destined to pass away, for depressions are not eternal any more than eclipses are, and in spite of man's imprudent remedies which usually retard recovery, they do pass in the end when Nature liquidates them in her own way. The world crisis, which was let loose in 1929 and has now proved to be definitely cyclical in character, is rapidly being left behind, and the market for Canadian wheat is becoming healthier.

According to the Stanford Food Research Institute the world production of wheat (Russia excepted) declined in the six years 1930-36 to a figure 500 million bushels below world consumption (if we include Russia the figure would be 240 millions). Although consumption declined during this period, production declined still more, and, if we believe the experts, there is now no real overproduction of cereals. The annual production of wheat in 1931-33 was still higher than it was in 1909-13, 120 million tons against 103. The amount of maize was about the same, 104 against 103, but barley, oats, and rye declined to a marked degree, 36 against 39, 60 against 67, and 40 against 49 million tons. This gives us an annual average of 361 million tons of cereals for 1909-13 and only 360 million for 1931-33.[1]

The economic section of the League of Nations confirms this theory in its report for 1934-35: "The world's population continues to increase at the rate of some 1.2 per cent a year, or perhaps more, and there is no reason to believe that habits of consumption have changed violently during the past year. The amount of food and agricultural raw materials produced in 1934 was less than in any year since 1927, though the population has increased meanwhile by perhaps 8 per cent to 10 per cent." Perhaps under such conditions we should no longer take the depression into account when we reason, and yet the accumulated ruins are still visible, and its lessons are so fresh in the mind that they still have con-

[1] Figures published by G. J. S. Broomhall of Liverpool.

siderable influence. These lessons must not be entirely forgotten, although everyone will be only too ready to do so as soon as better times return.

§ 2

Without being too much influenced by passing events, or forgetting the lessons of the crisis, let us now try to analyse the position of the Canadian wheat grower and the dangers which threaten him.

Our attention is immediately drawn to the question of price, for Canada being an exporter, depends upon the trend of the international wheat market. Actually its fluctuations were the determining factor in causing the booms of the war and the post-war periods, and also the recent depression. The price per bushel, which was about a dollar on the eve of the war, rose to almost two dollars from 1915-19. It remained at an average of $1.50 between 1920 and 1930, but fell in 1933 to $.60. Although it has advanced in 1936 to about $1.40, we must bear in mind that, owing to the depreciation of the Canadian dollar, this figure corresponds to only about $.84 in gold.

The price of land naturally follows these fluctuations. Since the beginning of the century one can distinguish two real estate booms, one coinciding with a wave of immigration and culminating in the years 1910-11, and the other after the war and continuing until about 1928.

Land values in these periods touched $100 an acre, but the depression brought them down to $5 an acre in so far as any sales at all could be made. In some years and in certain cases land was worth nothing at all.

Such figures and their wide variations are all we need to understand the North American mentality. I include the Canadians in this, for they are just as imprudent, just as easily carried away, and have the same dangerous weaknesses. Tell me the price of a bushel of wheat—the gold price—and whether the market is going up or down, and I can tell you all there is to know about the prosperity of the West, and its prospects for the immediate future. The market trend is more important than the actual quotation, for a high price indicates less than a rising price, just as a low price means less than a falling one. What really matters is that the rising tide is irresistibly bearing up the whole system. Then sales and exports are easy, and interest on loans is met so readily that no one even thinks about it. But if the level of the waters is receding and one touches bottom, everything is difficult, and loans contracted on a prosperity basis become intolerably heavy.

Now borrowing in these new communities is very general. People borrow to get themselves established, to buy a farm or round it off, to set themselves up with equipment, to build a house, to pay for a motor car, or to treat themselves to a trip! Whether it is necessary

or not, such is the custom. In America everyone borrows, especially in the West, immigrants and old colonists alike, Anglo-Saxons and French Canadians—the
latter perhaps less than the rest, though I am not so
sure! In this respect America, be it North or South, is
one and the same continent. When it comes to mortgag-
ing land, the United States or Canada are not very different from the Argentine or Chile. This characteristic
does not belong to any particular race or class. It is continental, and applies to the New World perhaps just
because it is new!

Borrowing explains not only the depression, but also
the catastrophic proportions it assumed in the Canadian
West. The entire edifice of prosperity had been constructed on a high price level believed to be permanent.
But what banker, what money-lender, can hope to carry
on when he has advanced, say, 50 per cent on collateral,
and that collateral later depreciates by three-quarters?
Such conditions cannot, indeed should not, continue.
And then this is by no means the whole story, for in the
Canadian West we are dealing with a single crop system run by people who are not peasants.

In most of Saskatchewan and part of Alberta almost
nothing but wheat is cultivated. Around Regina the
countryside, if such it may be termed, reveals this. I recall farmhouses built of wood and standing out in the
middle of bare fields—isolated houses like seaside bun-

galows with a few sheds for the machines and motor cars, theoretically protected by a few miserable trees which cannot flourish owing to the wind. The better ones have a kitchen garden, but most of them do not. This farmer has no poultry, no cows, no vegetables. Far from going periodically to market to sell his produce, he goes to town to buy food, usually in tins! He sells his crop and is paid for it all at once at harvest time, and the rest of the year has no income. If a depression comes along he is penniless, unless he has some savings salted away in the bank. But people do not economize much in the New World. He becomes a charge on the State, which must support him as one of the unemployed. In France, when a city man gets into difficulties, if he has kept in touch with the country, he goes back there, because when all else fails, the farm, he thinks, will still provide enough to eat. In the Canadian West recent experience has proved that in times of extreme crisis people could die of hunger on a farm. It is the defeated farmer who falls back on the city as his line of retreat.

It is a splendid country for wheat growing, one of the finest in the world, but two mistakes made in developing it have forced its people to suffer cruelly. First, it has been given up almost entirely to a single crop, without taking into consideration the fact that success depends upon exporting freely. They should have realized that the international market might fail them, as actually has been the case. Secondly, the high price of wheat has tempted them to cultivate ground which was not suitable. The climate here is marvellous for growing wheat, but as we travel westwards, especially along the American frontier, rainfall becomes irregular, and in places is insufficient. The meteorological charts show an entire zone where less than 20 inches fall annually, not to mention the years of drought, which are as severe as the biblical one in Joseph's Egypt. When the prairies still existed in their natural state, the buffalo grass held the soil together. Now, after a few years of cultivation, if the crop is a failure, the soil pulverizes and is carried away by the wind in a storm of dust. Where the top soil is thin, there is nothing left. The Indians and the early missionaries considered it unwise to plough up certain districts which should be kept as grassland, and, after witnessing the disastrous drought which took place in 1933 and 1934 most agricultural experts are of the same opinion. But the American, as we have already said, believed that he could break the bonds that linked him with Nature, and exceed the limits that the Indians in their wisdom had imposed long ago.

The Canadian West was harder hit by the depression than any other part of North America. The country stretching from the Great Lakes to the Rockies had aroused glowing hopes ever since the beginning of the twentieth century, but we must recognize the truth and consider what really can be expected. Nothing is more dangerous in a period of prosperity than to discount the future too liberally, and, in the same way, the risk of over-depreciation during a crisis is equally great. Having gained experience by going to both extremes, it should at last be possible today to understand the mistakes that were made during the past thirty years in the development of the Western Provinces.

When the construction of the Canadian Pacific Railway opened up this region to colonization in the last fifteen years of the nineteenth century, and then after 1900 when immigration spread like a wave over the prairie, the West was built up on the basis of extensive cultivation of wheat. The farms were very large, being 160, 320, or even 640 acres. As there was plenty of room to spread out freely, the advantages of concentration never occurred to anyone. If the 290,000 farms in the prairies had been grouped more closely together, the present agricultural population could easily have been fitted into a territory the size of Manitoba.

The system of scattered settlements has had serious consequences, social, political, and financial; in fact the destiny of the whole country has been affected. Because the farms were dispersed over an apparently limitless territory, it became necessary to build an excessive structure to keep the great body together. More railways were needed, and more roads; more administrative units had to be set up, more provinces and more capitals, which meant more public buildings, more houses of parliament, more cities. In short, the West was conceived on too ambitious a scale, a scale which, though entirely justified so long as prosperity continued, proved terribly heavy to maintain at low tide.

In America they see things big. When business is good the rosy future seems to justify any risk. Today in Canada there seems to be too much of everything. Three continental railways were thrown out across this country just before the war. They were still being equipped after peace was signed, in fact even when the crisis was already looming up. Enormous hotels rose at every important railway junction, and at others not so important. Calgary, with its 83,000 inhabitants, possesses a palace built by the C.P.R. which is larger and more luxurious than any provincial hotel in France. Vancouver has two palaces, but as the second was completed only after the depression had set in it still remains, at the time of writing, unopened. The luxury of the parliament buildings, of the city halls, of the post offices, of the schools, in fact of institutions of every kind, is extraordinary. One feels that the standard of life has been established on the basis of the top price of wheat. The equipment weighs down the economic structure, since it is too late to change it and difficult even to reduce it. These magnificent buildings must be kept up, and these streets must be paved. These railway lines—threatened today by the automobile and tomorrow by the aeroplane—cannot be allowed to perish. As a result public administration is excessively costly, and its costliness is reflected by heavy taxes, often uncollectable, and by defaults on the part of the municipalities and even the provinces.

Let us not be too eager to condemn, but simply say, as they do in America, that development has advanced too quickly. Yet the structure, as it exists today, appears to be unjustified until a system of international trade has been established—or re-established—which will make Canada permanently a great exporter of wheat. Otherwise there was perhaps a gleam of wisdom in the sulky remark of the Canadian who described the enormous effort in the West as "a complete civilization where there should be only buffalo grass"!

We find the same lavish imprudence in the way in which the farms have been developed. The farmers who established themselves on these wheat fields, the finest in the world, took it for granted that the export market would never fail them. It was obvious that the domestic consumption could not absorb more than a third of the crop. As the soil was good, and as prices reached an undreamed-of level, they were tempted into specialized cultivation. Machinery was constantly being perfected and there seemed to be no limit to efficient intensification. This trend was consistent with the American genius, but at the same time, like all things human, it followed the line of least resistance.

This kind of farming is not a mode of living, but a means of making money. In their haste to get rich, these colonists simply "mined the land" as they say in the West. Their methods, semi-industrial and performed with excellent technique, required only a few periods of intense work at seed time and harvest, leaving them between whiles plenty of liberty to run around in their motor cars or take an express train to Florida or California. The truth is that, apart from the mechanical aspect, these "miners of the land" are not interested in country life. They believe that they can eliminate it almost entirely. The time has come when agricultural machinery has made them free from their former dependence on hired labour. Their wives and daughters, especially if they have had a good "American" education, refuse to take care of the garden, the chickens and the farmyard. The farmer himself cannot be bothered with keeping livestock in addition to his wheat, for animals are a nuisance.

"What, no cows?" exclaimed a French Canadian visiting the West, to a farmer who confined his efforts to wheat. "You would balance your books better if you had a few."

"I leave that to someone else," was the reply. "When

I lived down East I had plenty of cows. I know all about them, and I am through!"

During the "fat" years the West, thinking of nothing but wheat, was determined to get a full year's profit out of three months' work, although in the East men with mixed farms were ready to work for twelve months for much the same result. There is something unhealthy about this western view which cannot last. The divorce from the soil has been made easy by the progress in communications. The automobile has played a tremendous part in the evolution of America, as no doubt will be appreciated in the future. It keeps people from taking root, for anyone can move on if he wants to. Apart from the fact that the wheat farmers are called agriculturists, they have little in common with the traditional farmer, who is wedded by love or interest, or perhaps both, to the soil he cultivates.

That there is something vicious about this system is revealed by the fact that it cannot stand up to a depression. The price of wheat when it is high can easily cover the cost of machinery, and justify the farmer's scale of living. It permits him to adopt industrial standards of mass production. But when the bottom drops out of the market, the burden of overhead becomes positively crushing. This is fatal to the farmer, who literally dies of starvation on his own farm from which, apart from the one product which has failed him, he can draw nothing whatsoever. What a paradox that the countryside should be forced to turn to the city for its food! There are certain factors in the overhead charges which are excessive and which cannot be adapted to a time of crisis. The first is the land itself, which has generally been bought at too high a price, and, secondly, the interest charges on the loans which were contracted to acquire it. Lastly, the agricultural machinery has also been too costly. The whole standard of living is too pretentious; it makes the struggle against more modest competitors far too difficult.

There is more resistance in the regions devoted to mixed farming, where something of the peasant tradition has been preserved. These are not only French Canadians by any means, for the Ontario farmers seem to have succeeded in combining the qualities of both Europe and America. Even in the West, the district bordering the wheat belt on the north suffered far less than the prairies. There one finds vegetable gardens and cattle instead of wheat, and thoroughbred horses alongside agricultural machinery. Experience has taught the money-lenders that mixed farming is more worthy of credit. There is a banker in Calgary, so they say, who will not grant a mortgage until he has satisfied himself that the farmer possesses horses! I often heard the idea expressed, in the regions devastated by the depression, that they should bring in or create a peasant class who, being more stable, would succeed even when the market declined. But, they added, the peasant would have to avoid getting into debt, make his family work, and not indulge in more luxury than the countryside could afford.

At Regina I was told of a significant conversation between two farmers. One said his cost price was $1.15 per bushel, and that he was losing money. He explained that with two cars and his daughter at the university he could not carry on any longer. The other, however, seemed to be succeeding. He was selling his wheat at the market rate and making a profit of 35 cents. He was a Ukrainian, and his methods were the same as those of any other European peasant. He lived modestly and was not in debt. The first man no doubt was technically superior, but the university and the two motor cars lay like a dead weight in the cost price of his bushel of wheat!

Thus the peasant survives, for, protected by his very simplicity, he bends like a reed in the storm. The "land miner," if he fails, founders, disappears, and becomes city proletariat. Though he sometimes manages to preserve his property it is in appearance only, for he is thenceforth dominated by powerful interests such as the bank, the railway, and the grain elevator. He hates them, and tries to defend himself by linking up politically with others in a similar plight.

Nevertheless he has been prosperous during two generations and prosperity seems once more on the point of returning. There is no reason to assume that the recent depression represents a normal condition likely to last, or is a permanent low level to be accepted with resignation. Yet this very pre-depression prosperity contained elements that were both precarious and exceptional. Borne up first by a rising tide of immigration, and then by the adventure of war, the West had all the dynamic energy of a region which was still being opened up. Today's success was due, to a great extent, to the active preparation for tomorrow, or to the discounting of future prosperity. It was a question of development rather than of a steady equilibrium. Perhaps, as Clemenceau once said, the normal condition was movement.

I cannot refrain from pondering on the contrast between the Western Canadian farmer's superior technique, which commands our admiration, and the need for a wiser attitude towards life and its possibilities. This sort of lesson has been handed down to us in the fables of every age, as part of the wisdom of nations— but America was inclined at first to turn aside from such wisdom. She liked to think that such platitudes did not apply to a young continent with a future still before it. Firmness has reappeared in the market price of wheat. Should this rising tide continue seriously, she will be ready once more to believe it all over again, and to forget the wisdom of the ages.

CHAPTER IX

INDUSTRY

§ 1

THE study of Canada's natural resources and her manufacturing development immediately raises a problem of considerable magnitude, viz., the degree of industrial processing which a country, at a given moment in its evolution, is capable of applying to the natural products of its soil. In this respect countries seem to vary in age. Some are young, for they export their raw materials without transforming them; others are old—adult, if you prefer—for they on the contrary import raw materials in order to manufacture and re-export them as finished products; others, again, are at a transition stage, exporting their products after only a partial processing, or possibly manufacturing them completely for their home markets alone. In which class shall we put Canada?

The essential characteristics of her natural resources are their richness, their immeasurable volume (the extent of Canada's reserves is hardly suspected even to-day), and their youth, by which I mean the margin still waiting to be exploited. In the United States, after squandering raw materials for several generations, they are beginning to realize that a time will come when this margin, in so far as certain products are concerned, will finally be exhausted. But in Canada they still talk of "unlimited" possibilities, and, moreover, they have every right to do so. They have three principal resources, each capable of "unlimited" exploitation: wheat, timber, and a whole series of minerals.

After studying the wheat situation, we are beginning to wonder if this abundance is an unmixed blessing. "What shall we do with it?" the Canadians sometimes say to themselves. The wealth is there nevertheless, and it would be foolish to pretend that they would be better off without it.

In 1933 forest products represented 6.72 per cent of the net value of the national production. The forests cover 1,153,000 square miles, a third of the area of the country. In extent this is greater than Russia in Europe, even with the addition of Sweden and Finland. Three-quarters can be utilized, and though depletion is not quite counterbalanced by annual growth, yet these resources can certainly be considered as inexhaustible. The map shows three distinct forests: One in the east, in Quebec, Ontario and the Maritime Provinces, consisting mainly of pine, maple, and birch; a second in the north, with birch, spruce, maple, and trees belonging to the cypress family; and a third on the Pacific coast,

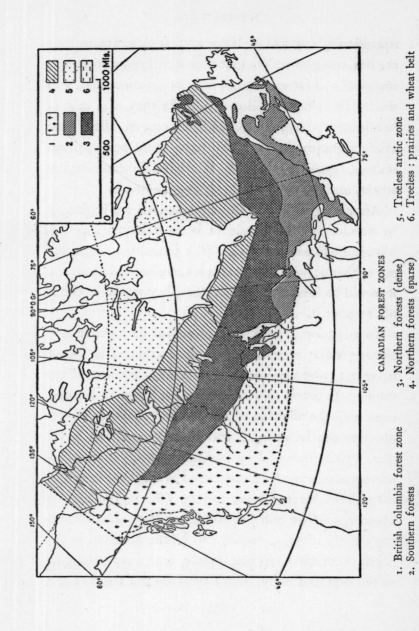

CANADIAN FOREST ZONES

1. British Columbia forest zone
2. Southern forests
3. Northern forests (dense)
4. Northern forests (sparse)
5. Treeless arctic zone
6. Treeless : prairies and wheat belt

composed of coniferous trees which are celebrated for their beauty. The Eastern Provinces contain 64 per cent of the accessible timber, British Columbia 24 per cent and the Prairie Provinces 12 per cent. One receives a lasting impression of reserves.

The mines represent 10.74 per cent of the net value of the country's total production. They must be classified before timber and water power, but far behind agriculture, for the latter accounts for 28.18 per cent. Nevertheless these minerals stand for something far more important than this apparently mediocre percentage indicates. Because of their future prospects they have acquired for Canada a position of special prestige in international financial circles. This has been of considerable assistance in her recent development. The following table summarizes her present position as a producer of minerals:

Mineral	Per Cent of World Production	Canada's Rank
Nickel	90	first
Asbestos	60	first
Cobalt	53	second
Copper	13	second
Gold	12	second or third
Zinc	15	third
Lead	12	third
Silver	10	third

This mineral wealth is found chiefly in the provinces of Ontario, Quebec, and British Columbia. Recent developments and future possibilities are, however, attracting attention to the North. It should be noted that the above table applies entirely to non-ferrous metals. This fact is not without interest, for it sheds a light on the formation of the economic personality of Canada. Although iron ore does not figure in our list, it is not because there is none, but simply that it is cheaper to import it from the United States. This has prevented Canada from acquiring her independence in the heavy industries.

In so far as fuel and power are concerned, a similar observation must be made regarding both coal and oil. Considerable reserves of coal exist, but they are located at the geographical extremes of the country, in Nova Scotia, Alberta, and British Columbia. In view of the immense distances across the country from east to west, it is to the interests of each region to import from the corresponding region in the United States, more especially as the greater part of the Canadian population is spread along the frontier. Out of an average consumption of 30 million tons (omitting the depression) 12 to 15 million are supplied by the country itself, and almost the entire balance is imported from its great neighbour. The same applies to oil, for although production is far from negligible, it is as yet of no great importance.

On the contrary, with hydro-electric power we return

to the domain of "infinite possibilities." The unde-veloped power resources are immense, 20 million h.p. at ordinary minimum flow of which 7½ millions are already being utilized by power stations. This gives Canada second rank in the world, coming after the United States, but first, if we calculate the *per capita* output. This brings us back to the Laurentians, as they play the leading role owing to their glacial formation. Thanks to their innumerable lakes which act as natural reservoirs, and to the hundreds of rivers where deep sluggish stretches are followed by rapids, the water is first stored up and then suddenly let loose. Hydro-electric energy thus accounts for 98 per cent of the country's production of electricity. The Rocky Moun-tains and the Northwest also have waterfalls enough to satisfy countries less richly endowed, but it is the provinces of Quebec, Ontario, and Manitoba that are the most important, for they are flanked by the Lauren-tian Shield. This vast area, which at first appears sterile and devoid of hope, is thus a source of potential wealth which has never yet been estimated. In the nineteenth century, when coal and the steam engine dominated the world, the Laurentians seemed of little or no value, but in the present age of electricity, Canada possesses in them a priceless advantage, perfectly adapted to the needs of our time.

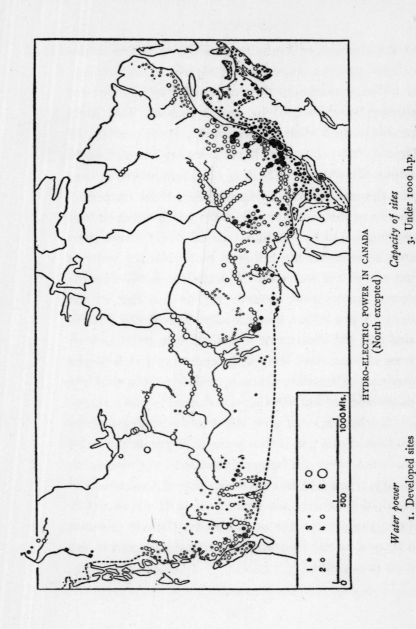

HYDRO-ELECTRIC POWER IN CANADA
(North excepted)

Water power

1. Developed sites
2. Undeveloped sites

Capacity of sites

3. Under 1000 h.p.
4. 1000 h.p. to 100,000 h.p.
5. 100,000 h.p. to 1,000,000 h.p.
6. Over 1,000,000 h.p.

1 ●   3 ·   5 ○
2 ○   4 ○   6 ○

0   500   1000 Mls.

§ 2

Given this background, what sort of industrial production are we likely to find? It is a big subject, extending beyond the Canadian borders and really embracing the whole question of the industrialization of young countries overseas. In the simple economic equilibrium of the nineteenth century, the New World exported foodstuffs and raw materials, and hardly thought of using anything but imported manufactured goods for their own needs. Today these adolescents are emancipating themselves, and are now contesting the remnants of the colonial pact—remnants which amounted to much more than was realized at the time. How far are they justified for example in setting up permanent industries of their own? Has Canada normally reached the stage of industrialization? Can she maintain it? If so, in which branches of production?

We must first consider the amount of motive power and raw materials at her disposal. In an age of steam she would be badly placed, for her coal beds, as we have said, are located at her extreme edges. Coal mines in Alberta are about as useful to Eastern Canada as the Donetz Basin is to France. But water power abounds, especially on the edge of the Laurentian Shield, and it is so easily transported that it can be used anywhere and at low cost. As for raw materials, she possesses wood and cereals in profusion, and, like the poetic land of Cipango, the North, with its far-off mines, abounds in various metals. Having said this much, however, we have come to the end of the "unlimited resources." They are not very varied in type, for they are severely limited by the northern climate. If necessary the mining of iron ore might be developed, and also the production of wool, but neither cotton nor silk, nor indeed any of the other principal colonial products are to be found in these parts. They can easily be imported, you will say. True, but owing to the geographic disposition of the continents and the direction of the existing trade routes, England, with the *entrepôt* market of London at her disposal, is in a better position than British North America for securing the raw materials which industry requires.

Another limitation results from the mediocrity of the Canadian home market. It may seem strange to use such a term in connection with a country with an area of three and a half million square miles, but one must not forget that it contains not more than ten million inhabitants. Even taking into account a relatively high purchasing power *per capita*, Canada is at a grave disadvantage when she launches into industrialization. Any hope of mass production vanishes as there are not sufficient consumers inside the tariff walls. Therefore output cannot be standardized, nor can the specialization of the various factories in the same industry be carried to its maximum. They are thus condemned to a diversified type of production, which is costly. Exports can be considered, but only at the international price level, which presupposes either dumping, which is difficult to continue for long, or else concentration on certain industries where advantages exist. This introduces another limitation.

The Canadian market does benefit, however, from one exceptional advantage—paid for, it is true, by serious risks—in her close proximity to the United States. The word proximity is hardly strong enough, for the two countries have a common economic atmosphere and are, in this respect, both the same country. The attraction exerted by the 130 million people to the south is irresistible. Such conditions exist nowhere else in the world, for neither the economic intimacy between France and Belgium or Switzerland, nor that between Austria and Germany, can begin to compare with the familiarity between Canada and the United States. No form of protection has ever succeeded in impairing it seriously. Canada manifestly profits by it, for she participates without effort on her own part in the magnificent vitality of her neighbour. Any technical progress achieved in the United States is immediately extended to her; she benefits from their equipment, their capital, and their technical experts, as if they were her own.

Were it not for the tariff, there might as well be no frontier, and if a regime of free trade were established, the customs union would open up possibilities of economic development which would literally be incalculable.

The reverse of the medal is that the Canadians, in spite of themselves, inherit a costly mode of living, as one does when sharing a flat with a wealthy friend. The Canadians must keep up to the mark or lose their population by migration across the border. This is no mere supposition, as their chronic emigration has abundantly proved. The American atmosphere has a direct repercussion on Canadian tastes, habits, wage level, and conditions of work, all of which inflate the cost of production just as they do in the United States, where, except when mass production enters in, costs naturally tend to be high. In order to defend herself against her giant brother, Canada is almost bound to become Americanized. In any case she is always threatened with becoming a mere annex. Any other development is, I do not say impossible, but artificial. Once again the *leitmotiv* of the North-South axis comes into play.

One might think that such conditions might benefit her industrial equipment, for she is able to make use of the finest technical experts in the world, not to mention those now being trained along similar lines in the Canadian universities, and she can order in the neigh-

bouring market any machinery or machine-tools required. This would be the case if it were not for a
double handicap. In the first place there is the tariff,
which Canada herself chooses to erect, but which perhaps is necessary if she is to keep her individuality; and
secondly her climate, which requires solidly built factories, with thick walls and roofs strong enough to support the weight of the snow.

The same applies to labour, for here again contradictory factors come into play. We must be like a canny
Normandy peasant who refuses to make a direct statement for fear of compromising himself. Let us say that,
on a continent where wages are high, Canadian wages
are, by comparison, not unduly so; but that they are
high when one thinks of Europe. The French Canadians must be placed in a separate category, for owing
to their excessive birth-rate, and the way they are drifting into the towns, they constitute an abundant supply
of relatively cheap labour. Capital is glad to employ
them, for they are docile, and disciplined by their priests
according to a tradition which belongs neither to their
continent nor to the present day.

Otherwise labour in Canada is generally about 40
per cent dearer than in England, but cheaper than in
the United States. The rate is about $4 a day, and $6
for skilled workers, the figure sometimes falling to
$2.50 or $2 in the small manufacturing towns of the

lower St. Lawrence. Thus, in comparison with Europe the Canadian workman is expensive. Added to this we must not forget that extra winter costs have to be compensated for in the wage level. Generally speaking the Canadian workman has adopted the standards of the New World, for he arrives at the factory in his car, wears gauntlets at work, is well equipped and well housed. Often he is a member of the American Federation of Labour, which frequently obtains for him, in spite of the frontier, the same advantages that he would have in the United States. The social standard of the whole continent, or shall we say the standard of living, is definitely American.

§ 3

When we value Canada's bridge hand, we find that she holds a few marvellous trumps—economic youth, and practically unlimited water power and raw materials. But there are weak cards too—the small home market, and the proximity of the United States, resulting in a high standard of living and inflated costs of production. Owing to her natural wealth, Canada is bound to figure among the great international producers. This is her strong point in her relations with both the United States and Europe, and no one can take it from her. But again there is a double handicap, for, not being able to adopt mass production owing to her small population, she cannot compete with the United States, nor even imitate her except under artificial conditions. Having an American wage level, it is also difficult for her to struggle against European or even English labour, which is more modestly remunerated. We therefore conclude that Canada will succeed better in industries where raw materials and water power are the principal requirements, but that the further one goes up the manufacturing scale, the more her advantages tend to disappear. Industrial development is possible therefore only under relatively artificial conditions, and only to a limited extent.

In the light of these remarks, let us now classify the Canadian industries into three main groups. The first comprises those which produce under the best conditions as regards costs and therefore can compete internationally with anyone. These are, generally speaking, industries carrying out the first stage of transformation only, and producing semi-finished products. They are mainly industries which benefit either from an abundance of raw materials on the spot or easily imported, or else those that depend on large quantities of cheap hydro-electric power available where needed. When these conditions are fulfilled, common sense suggests processing the raw materials only to the point of semi-manufacture, and then exporting them. These are the true Canadian industries, which should logically be developed in Canada. Pulp, paper, aluminium, and all forms of electro-metallurgy and electro-chemistry come under this category. Geographically they tend to be located less according to the source of their motive power which is transportable, than at the geometric centre to which their raw materials can be easily brought and from which their products can be conveniently shipped or exported to the consuming centres. We may assume that, owing to the favourable circumstances under which they are evolving, these industries should be able to hold their place against international competition, for high wages make little difference as abundant water power is the essential factor.

The real test is their ability to export. This is clearly indicated in the following list of the most important industries in the first group: [1]

Product	Per Cent of Total Output Sold Abroad
Pulp	66 in 1908, 16 in 1934
Newsprint	92 in 1934
Paper	71 in 1934
Spirits	63 in 1929
Lead	66 in 1929
Zinc	77 in 1929
Artificial manures	75 in 1919

In the second group we shall place industries which turn out finished products, such as woollen and cotton textiles.

[1] The Canadian Government believes in exporting forest products in as highly manufactured a state as possible.

These derive no advantage from local raw materials, and can defend themselves against foreign competition only by a tariff. It is not that they are unsound, but that they cannot prosper except in an artificial atmosphere. They work almost exclusively for the home trade, and their initial weakness lies in the smallness of their market. This is particularly striking in the case of cotton manufacturers, who cannot adopt methods of mass production, because their local clientele is so exacting that they are obliged to offer a varied range. This is a drawback for which no other element in the cost price can compensate. Their machinery is excellent, often ultramodern, but it is expensive, as duty has to be paid when it comes into the country. Labour is relatively dear in comparison with Manchester, where, in addition, the weavers and the spinners are probably more highly skilled. The bill for raw materials is rather heavier than in Lancashire, for though cotton must be imported to the banks of the St. Lawrence the same as to the Mersey, the British *entrepôt* market, by handling it in enormous quantities, can furnish it more cheaply to their own textile mills.

In short, Canada can undertake to manufacture cotton textiles and may even succeed in doing so, but she cannot withstand international competition. She dare not expose herself even to English competition without some defence, so any concession or preferential tariff is immediately resented. This evidently marks a point in imperial policy beyond which the Dominion cannot pass without sacrifice. Therefore this industrial group, which is established in the East, must be considered artificial, almost exotic. This does not mean that it should not survive, but simply that it soon encounters an implacable limit, due in reality to its inability to export. Even in the prosperous year of 1929, the percentage of production exported in these industries remained extraordinarily low: 0.6 per cent for cottons, 0.7 per cent for woollens, and 7 per cent for ready-made garments.

A third and rather numerous group of industries which is particularly interesting to study includes those which on closer examination prove to be merely branches of American industry. These belong to mass production enterprise on an enormous scale, with headquarters in the United States, but which have been established in Canada within the tariff barrier in order to have access to the Canadian market, and also to enjoy the preferences reserved for the Dominion in the rest of the Empire. Such enterprises have no really autonomous existence in Canada. Their technical operations are carried out there certainly, but all effective inspiration and direction come from across the border. The progress made in cutting down their costs through mass production becomes possible in a country with a small population, only because they depend less on the Cana-

dian economic background than on the advantage of par-
ticipating in a much larger market. Their manufacturing plans and designs are drawn up by specialists in
centralized offices in the United States. Many individual
parts are made at Detroit or Chicago, according to ultra-
standardized and highly economical models, and are
then assembled in the factory in Quebec or Ontario.
The same applies to the allocation of territories market-
wise and to the organization of production. Everything
is decided in the spirit of a cartel, by an arbitrary authority at a distance beyond the frontier.

Such enterprises, although registered under Canadian
statute and having Canadian personnel—I shall not
dwell on the origin of their capital—may be considered
as branches of a parent house. I would say of a foreign
parent house if the two occupants of the North American continent could really be considered foreign to each
other. These industries vary in their dependence on the
United States. Motor cars and pneumatic tyres are important examples, and agricultural machinery, but the
latter only to a certain extent, for the Massey Harris
Company is purely Canadian. Almost all are situated
in the provinces of Quebec and Ontario, notably on
the shores of Lake Erie and Lake Ontario. Here again
we find an important export capacity. In 1929 the automobile industry exported 35 per cent of its production,
the tyre industry 39 per cent, and agricultural ma-

chinery 51 per cent. If we count Canada as an exporter
in this instance, most of the credit must be given to the
larger entity of North America.

§ 4

In 1929 the principal Canadian industries, classified
according to the net value of their production, appeared in the following order:

	Per Cent of Total Production
Foodstuffs, and industries derived from agriculture	23
Wood, pulp, and paper	20
Iron, steel, and heavy industries	15
Minerals and metals	14
Textiles	10
Electric power	6
Chemical industries	4

Geographically manufacturing is carried on mainly
in the East. The Province of Ontario furnishes nearly
half the value of the industrial production, and Quebec
about one-third. Actually it is in this part of the country, between the Great Lakes and the Laurentians, that
the necessary water power and labour is found, as well
as the most concentrated local market. The financial
centres of Montreal and Toronto are there too to provide the capital, and finally, it is situated close to the
greatest industrial region of the United States. Secondary groups occur in British Columbia, Manitoba, and

the Maritime Provinces, but we may be permitted to say that, generally speaking, the valley of the St. Lawrence at once makes one think of Canadian industrial activity.

It is important to note that the three groups of industries analysed above are all more or less equal in importance to Canada. The first is important because it relies upon the natural resources with which the country has been especially blessed; the second because its success depends upon the deliberate policy of the country, and because it is linked up with the development of the East; and the third, because it brings the Dominion into close participation in the life of the United States. I feel that Canada can hardly abandon any of these three groups without seriously impairing herself, for each one in its own way is bound up with her personality. In the first place we naturally think of the development of a young country, which is exploiting its resources and normally exporting them after they have passed the first stage of manufacture, which can be carried out better on the spot than anywhere else. In the second case there is the determination which invariably exists in countries on the road to maturity to become as complete and diversified as possible, by manufacturing as much of their own needs as they can. Finally in the third case we find a circumstantial development due more to neighbouring than to internal initiative, which introduces into the national life a ferment of intense activity and progress.

Owing to the diversity of these elements, the economic life of Canada is singularly complex. It involves not only continental relationships, but imperial and international as well, which raise the Dominion to a position in the world far exceeding that which the modest figure of her population would justify.

CHAPTER X

CURRENCY, FINANCE AND FOREIGN TRADE

§ 1

LET us begin by taking a bird's-eye view of the development of Canada during the past half century. At first, up to 1896 or 1900, progress was slow. The West was still empty, although preparations for its settlement were under way. British Columbia, the Ultima Thule of America, seemed infinitely far off and scarcely connected with the rest of the country. Even at that time Canada still lay entirely in the East, between the Atlantic and the Great Lakes, as had been the case before Confederation. This tardy growth may have been due to the cycle of falling prices which from 1873 to 1896 had disheartened the whole world. At any rate it was not until the century had run its course that Canada's splendid expansion took place, first with immigration, as we have seen, and then with wheat. As the West developed, and as the transcontinental railways brought settlers to the prairies and opened up three new provinces to agriculture, Canada became no longer a mere succession of scattered colonies, but a country of magnificent dimensions, stretching from coast to coast.

This sudden spurt, which was greatly admired at the time, was made possible by the financial support given by Great Britain in the true imperial manner. On the eve of the war two-thirds of the foreign capital invested in Canada was British. Furthermore the movement towards the west was canalized, or at least intensified, by the American policy of protection. The McKinley tariff was imposed in 1890, the Dingley tariff in 1897, and the Payne-Aldrich tariff in 1909. The British and Canadian wave which spread over the prairies was prevented from overflowing to the south by the insurmount customs wall, although Nature might have intended the contrary. It almost seemed as if this policy of showing no consideration for a friendly neighbour had been purposely conceived by the White House to bind more closely the ties between Canada and England which had been slackening during the previous century. Actually Canada's first imperial preferential tariff was set up in 1897, and with its advent the dream of a continental customs union faded away, and the Canadian East was organized industrially to furnish the West with the equipment it required. In military parlance, it became the West's base. This is why the exceptional progress of the prairies was accompanied by a corresponding and no less remarkable progress in the old provinces of the St. Lawrence, which now served as stages or points of departure for the new exploitation out West.

This boom, for such it was, would no doubt have been followed by a serious depression, if a new period, beginning with the war, had not quite unexpectedly been inaugurated. By supplying the Allies with their needs, Canada was called upon to fill an international role. In 1914 and during the next four years, there was an insatiable demand for all kinds of agriculture and mining products at any price. Everything offered was snapped up immediately without discussion, and the seller was urged to send as much more as he could on any terms he chose to name. This stimulated a great expansion of production, which, in the case of wheat, as we have seen, was carried to extremes. As in the preceding phase, Canadian industry was also being correspondingly stimulated. The pressing needs of the belligerents were not only for foodstuffs and raw materials. They also wanted a whole series of manufactured articles for immediate use, such as armaments, munitions, tools, transport vehicles, etc.

Few countries outside of Europe were in a position to fill such demands, for it was necessary to have an industrial equipment already in existence, or at least the ability to create one without delay. The United States and Japan alone were ready to meet the emergency, but Canada came closely after as the third great industrial producer. In this case she benefited from her proximity to the United States, and from the atmosphere of the whole continent which permitted the second of its two countries to rise to the level of the first, thereby hastening its entry into industrialism. In addition to European orders for Canadian manufactured goods, the Canadian market itself began to make excessive demands. The West, enriched by its exports of wheat which gave it great purchasing power, clamoured for a host of industrial products, even luxuries, which the old continent at the moment was unable to deliver —and here also prices began to rise! The temptation was very great to create an industry which could profit by this extraordinary, almost unheard-of opportunity. With technique borrowed from the United States, that is exactly what Canadians did.

The question was how to finance this new effort. Under the circumstances Canada could not count as before on English capital, because it had all been requisitioned in Europe for the task of national defence. But the United States had suddenly become immensely enriched by the unexpected opportunity, and, by the same token, Canada herself had acquired an excess of liquid capital which she was able to invest in her own industries. Thus began a new phase in Canadian history. Of the total amount of foreign capital invested in the Dominion, England's share dropped between 1914 and

1919 from 71 per cent to 57 per cent, while that of the United States rose from 24 per cent to 39 per cent. The war thus had the effect of hastening Canada's economic maturity, and of weaning her away from British financial support. She became Americanized in the continental sense, or "dis-Europeanized," if I may coin the word, by a crisis which accentuated more than ever her New World characteristics. She increased her resemblance to, and her connection with, the United States by paralleling the latter's evolution in a striking way. The fact that she fought for the Empire on the battlefields made no difference whatsoever!

Once peace was re-established, and after the superficial shudder of the brief depression of 1920-21 which liquidated nothing, came a period of prosperity which lasted from about 1924 to 1929. This boom looked like a replica or prolongation of war fever. It should be classed as such, for it is inseparably bound up with the war period. Once again the fundamental elements are wheat exports at top prices to a Europe which was not yet reconstructed, the participation—almost physical —in the economic enthusiasm of the United States, and the purchasing power of the West, which once more provided the industry of the East with a magnificent internal market. To provide for this development fresh capital as usual had to be called in, and so foreign borrowings rose from $4,580,776,000 in 1919 to $5,892,-419,000 in 1929. But the origin of these loans shows that the modification in Canada's borrowing policy which had commenced in 1914 was continued. The following table leaves no doubt on this point:

Foreign Capital Invested in Canada [1]

	1919	1929
United States	$1,800,435,000	$3,608,521,000
England	2,606,848,000	2,128,489,000
Other Countries	173,493,000	155,409,000

While American capital was doubling itself, the volume of purely English capital declined by about one-fifth. The British share, which still in 1919 had been about 57 per cent, now fell to 36 per cent, as the American rose from 39 per cent to 61 per cent, for, as we have shown, the Dominion was becoming in a way an industrial section of the United States. But at this moment of incomparable expansion, neither the Americans nor the Canadians seem to have been aware that this economic tide had reached an exceptionally high-water mark.

The depression, alas, caught them all in the end. After Wall Street had crashed in 1929, and especially after the pound sterling went off gold in 1931, public opinion began to realize that what was happening was

[1] Estimates of the Dominion Bureau of Statistics.

the liquidation of the war. The whole world was equipped to provide for an exceptional consumption, which melted away when purchasing power was reduced to normal and permanent proportions. To quote Bismarck's expression, it was "time to put the clock right," but the time was the hour of penitence. Canada was directly hit. She had been living and profiting on her export trade. For the last twenty years she had founded her expansion first on the war and the needs of the belligerents, and then on the international market. The western wheat exporter, being in the vanguard, was the first to fall, and he dragged down with him the eastern industrialist, who could, of course, only fall back on the insufficient home market.

Such a reversal in the economic current was bound to alter many of the results of the previous high tide. One sees for example that since 1929 American influence has been declining, while British influence has reappeared. England has not given up, but is again having her say in financial and monetary matters. Indeed she may start again to provide capital, for the volume of her investments shows an increase from $2,-128,489,000 in 1929 to $2,204,857,000 in 1931. The Ottawa Conference in 1932 also marked a turning point, after which British imports into Canada increased. The prestige of the United States suffered terribly by this unprecedented depression, coming without warning after a period of economic glory that everyone believed would last for ever. English prestige, especially after the magnificent defence England put up in 1931, increased in like measure. Nevertheless, Canada is still situated in North America, and any other aspect of the Canadian problem is of secondary importance. In the end the current is bound to reverse and flow towards the U.S.A. In financial matters this is already apparent.

§ 2

The economic equilibrium of Canada has not been the same at each stage of her development, as is shown by her trade balance which reveals two main periods. The first, from 1904 to 1914, was unfavourable, as exports at that time did not amount to more than 75 per cent of imports. The opening up of the West meant the need of new equipment, most of which could be obtained only abroad. The result was an unfavourable balance of trade. As the country could not cover these imports by its exports, as it would have done in normal times, it was obliged to resort to foreign borrowing. This was the period of the great influx of British capital, which was simply the support that a young country has every right to expect from its mother. In this case England was, at the time, both rich beyond her own needs, and also still Canada's political sovereign.

The second period, from 1915 to 1935 (excepting

the three years of 1921, 1930, and 1931), showed on the contrary a series of favourable balances, corresponding to two prodigious spurts of prosperity in the war and the post-war years. From 1917 to 1920, it was imports which now represented only 70 per cent of exports, and in the economically homogeneous years from 1924 to 1929 the proportion was maintained at an average of 81 per cent.

These initial observations give us the clue to the character of the Canadian equilibrium. With an immense area but only a tiny population—what, after all, is ten million?—Canada obviously can produce far more than she can consume. For various reasons, however, she must import, and, although less than previously, she still must procure capital and equipment abroad. In addition, owing to her climate, tropical and sub-tropical commodities will always be lacking. Unless she resigns herself to a lower standard of living, she must import them, just as Europe does, only to an even greater extent. Under these conditions economic autarchy is an impossible dream. Exports, therefore, are urgently necessary, since they alone can compensate for Canada's three needs of capital, equipment, and natural products ripened in a kindlier climate. It is not surprising to find that in 1929 Canada came third, on a *per capita* basis, after New Zealand and Denmark, among the great exporting countries, with exports of

$136 per head of population, against only $43 for the United States.

This equilibrium is perilously vulnerable, for in the last analysis it depends upon, and is closely linked to, the international market, but yet has no effective influence over it. Also, there are two other causes of trouble. The first is that these indispensable exports are mainly of two classes only: wheat, of which three-quarters of her production must be liquidated abroad; and timber, where she is in a similar position, since three-quarters of her paper and nine-tenths of her newsprint are specially made for foreign consumption. The second difficulty is that, generally speaking, each of these two exports is shipped to a single customer, wheat to England, and forest products to the United States. Therefore she has no economic independence. She could have it, and it is always there in reserve against a rainy day, if she were willing to accept a standard of living below what we call civilization. The ten million Canadians, with their broad fertile lands and the resources of their forests and fisheries, assuredly will never die of starvation, which is more than the rest of us can say today. But if they wish to live above the log-cabin stage, or even above the peasant farm, they must rely on the precarious structure of an international system. Even though they have become politically sovereign, they will still depend either upon the international markets, or, more serious perhaps, on their own patrons, England and the United States.

The composition of Canadian imports will enlighten us as to the position in which the country finds itself when, far from renouncing modern civilization, she justly flatters herself on being in the front rank and on sharing in the high standard of living enjoyed by the United States. In 1934-35, during the depression, the greater part of her imports, actually about 70 per cent, were manufactured products (60 per cent finished and 9 per cent semi-finished). They were mainly metallurgical products and textiles. The remaining 30 per cent consisted of raw materials (coal, oil and raw cotton, rubber, etc.) and foodstuffs (fruit, sugar, tea, coffee, cocoa—the tropical commodities which will always be lacking). This list of imports, in which finished goods predominate, is typical of any young country which has not yet completely shaken off its dependence on foreign industry, as has the United States. In our comparisons with the past, even with the recent past, we discern a significant trend. Alongside these imports of manufactured goods, which were previously well in the lead, we now find a growing tendency to import raw materials to be manufactured within the country. This transition towards industrialism is clearly indicated in the statistics.

Quite apart from its volume, it is also essential for

us to ascertain the origin of Canada's import trade. The great source of supply is the United States, which in 1935 provided 58 per cent of Canada's total needs, especially manufactured goods, which made up 56 per cent of the total imports from the U.S.A. Metallurgical and mechanical goods predominated, but also certain combustibles and basic raw materials such as coal, oil, minerals, and raw cotton were important, due, no doubt, to their proximity. England comes second, but a long way after, with only 21 per cent. Her range is more specialized than that of the United States, being largely confined to manufactured goods, of which she supplied about one-third of Canada's requirements. Particularly important are the textiles which, of course, she distributes all over the world. By contrast Canada brings little from South America; about 75 per cent of her imports from this source consist of raw materials.

The United States evidently is the natural, inevitable, and almost statutory source of supply, even when treaties and laws are expressly drawn up to the contrary. How could it be otherwise, considering the close community of civilization that unites the two countries. They are like brother and sister. Their common mother is England, but the American continent is their nurse. The part played by the mother country in Canadian imports fell from 56 per cent of the total in 1870 to 15 per cent in 1930. The Ottawa agreements, combined with the effects of the depression, brought the proportion up to 24 per cent in 1934, and 21 per cent in 1935, as if a current of long duration had been reversed. But such re-establishment is precarious and contrary to the nature of things. It was arranged for the benefit of a country situated in another continent eight days away by sea, and it does not take into account a proximity which is more tyrannical in its effects than all the interventions which the ingenuity of politicians can devise. This is a case where the East-West trend cannot prevail against the North-South one.

Canada's exports confirm the same tendencies that we found in her imports. In the nineteenth century she spontaneously exported raw materials. This could not have been otherwise, in view of her economic youth in conjunction with the advanced age of Europe. Today we find her anxious to export semi-finished products. Instead of selling them abroad in their primary form, she wants to perform the first processes herself, and to push the system as far as logically possible. This aspiration is expressed less by tampering with customs duties, which are useless for that purpose, than by placing an embargo on certain exports. For example, Canada has prohibited the export of electric power, in order to attract or retain industries which otherwise would certainly establish themselves in the United States. Similarly she has forbidden the export of wood in its raw state from nationally owned timber limits, in order to force the seller to ship an article which is already partially worked, such as pulp or newsprint.

The development of the export of forest products is significant. The percentage of pulpwood exported amounted to 63 per cent in 1908, but partly as the result of an embargo which the Government of British Columbia put into force that year, and which other provinces also adopted, this figure was reduced to 48 per cent by 1913. Since then it fell to 19 per cent by 1929, and to 15 per cent by 1933. The aim, which was to put a brake on raw material exports, was thus fully achieved. We find the same tendency in pulp, another semi-finished product, as is shown by the following table:

Year	Proportion of Pulp Exported (Per Cent)
1908	66
1913	34
1929	20
1933	20

Unfortunately the statistics of the exports of paper are obtainable only after 1917, but we gather that they are moving logically in the opposite direction, as the figure reached 74 per cent in 1933. The tendency in the case of newsprint is even more marked:

Year	Proportion of Newsprint Exported (Per Cent)
1917	86
1929	92
1933	90
1934	92

It is difficult for statisticians to classify Canadian exports according to the exact degree of manufacture which the various commodities have undergone, but we may regard the following figures as approximate:

Products	Percentage of Exports, 1935
Raw materials	36
Semi-manufactures	21
Finished articles	43
	100

The following table also is interesting, as it subdivides the export trade according to another classification:

Products	Percentage of Exports, 1935
Cereals	26
Wood and its derivatives	24
Minerals and metals	23
Animal products	13
Other vegetable products	9
Sundry	5
	100

Such are the types of produce which Canada ships to the international markets. Now let us study their destinations.

If Canada's best source of supply is the United States, her best customer is England, who took 41 per cent of her exports in 1935. Half of these were raw materials, chiefly wheat. The Old Country's continued support is not astonishing, for it represents the survival of the nineteenth-century regime of complementary trade, when cottons and machinery were exchanged for cereals and raw materials. Though American industry has stolen away from its British competitor the greater part of the Canadian market, the mother country has continued up to the present to purchase her foodstuffs from the Dominion. The result is that Canada now sells England more than she buys from her.

The United States, on the contrary, took in 1935 only 34 per cent of her neighbour's exports, in this matter ranking second. The interesting observation here is that we are no longer dealing with complementary trade, but with an entirely different economic relationship. Because the continental intimacy is so complete, this trade is more like internal commerce. Canada seems to constitute, so far as the United States is concerned, a reserve of raw materials. Actually this is so, and furthermore, owing to their proximity, their resemblance, and the extent to which American capital is involved, a whole series of industrial operations is carried out behind the shelter of the Canadian tariff. The American purchaser thus imports finished articles which have been, in numerous instances, manufactured abroad by Americans, but the interests of the two countries are so intermingled that it is difficult to recognize what is American and what is Canadian.

Manufactured products account for 50 per cent of Canada's exports to the United States, and semi-finished for 23 per cent. This is not surprising when one considers that vegetable and animal products amount to only 28 per cent, whereas forest products, including paper, attain not less than 48 per cent. No matter what happens, no barrier will ever prevent these two economic units from communicating!

As we have seen, the two markets, English and American, absorb 75 per cent of Canadian exports. This means that the remaining 25 per cent is destined for other markets, notably, 10 per cent to the rest of the British Empire, and 8 per cent to Europe. We now have a fairly accurate idea of the relative importance of the country's various clients. The United States and England tie for first place (it would be tactless for a foreigner to award the first prize), but other countries, Europe in particular, also figure on the economic horizon. The international safety valve should be considered as an indispensable factor for Canada's independence.

§ 3

The Dominion Bureau of Statistics publishes estimates of the total investment of foreign capital in Canada in 1931 and 1934:

Foreign Investment in Canada (*ooo omitted*)

	1931		Jan. 1, 1934	
British	$2,204,857	or 34%	$2,734,197	or 40%
American	4,107,803	or 63%	3,983,231	or 59%
Other	165,217	or 3%	95,933	or 1%
Total	$6,477,879	100%	$6,813,361	100%

It is thus apparent that the depression in the U.S.A.
gave English finance the opportunity of regaining some
of the territory lost during the war.

We must not overlook the fact that foreign capital
in 1931 constituted only 15½ per cent of the national
wealth of the country, which in 1930 had been estimated at $30,840,210,000. It would be a gross exag-
geration to consider Canada as being possessed, or, to
use an American expression, controlled, by the United
States. During its two phases of great prosperity, it
seemed as if the country had succeeded in becoming an
accumulator of capital. This was proved by the fact that
during the war the people subscribed to two thousand
million dollars of Dominion Government bonds. Nevertheless Canada is always in need of foreign capital, so

that, even if this factor is not decisive it still remains a fundamental consideration, and must be borne in mind if we wish to understand Canadian policy.

British capital is invested chiefly in the railways; dominion, provincial, and municipal bonds; in land mortgage companies and in mining, these four groups representing 81 per cent in 1934. Britain's investments in Canada were made according to the same ideas that guided her in placing her capital all over the world in the nineteenth century. She supervises them as closely as possible, choosing her representatives judiciously and generally listening to their advice. This financial bond, which undoubtedly still has a political character, enables her to exert an influence which, though subtle, is effective. Her point of view is represented in a host of Canadian affairs which, although belonging to the New World, are thus tinted by English influence. We must not be misled by this survival. In spite of the reacquired prestige which the depression brought back to the mother country, to the detriment of Canada's colossal but erratic neighbour, British financial interest belongs to the past rather than to the future. This is especially so since capital no longer moves along the same currents as in preceding generations. The United States seems to be too close for the struggle to be equal; at best England might maintain the positions she has acquired, regaining perhaps a few lost trenches. But can anyone fight at the same time against both geography and the trend of the century?

American capital is being directed largely towards railroads, government loans, and public utility enterprises. These three types made up 61 per cent of the total in 1934, but their investment in industry—mines, timber, paper, motor cars, etc.—is also very important, amounting to 29 per cent. Actually in Canada the U.S.A. has more capital than England has in everything except railways and land mortgage companies:

Relative Amounts of Capital Invested in Canada, 1933

	United States (Per Cent)	Great Britain (Per Cent)
Government loans	66	33
Public utilities	75	23
Pulp and paper	79	20
Mines	59	39
Metal industries	80	18
Railroads	38	60
Mortgages	32	54

Nowhere else in the world has the United States such important assets, since her Canadian portfolio is three times as big as is her interest in any other country. The term "portfolio" is here not quite correct, for part of her Canadian assets are in directly owned properties. In other words it is less a question of subscribing to shares or bonds, than the creation of factories bought outright or constructed from the ground up, or of obtaining "control" of natural resources. On the one hand we have people who are looking for sound investments giving a good return; at the same time we also have American industry extending its hold over reserves of raw materials or acquiring markets for its goods.

Let us overlook for the moment the eventual danger of political control. Apart from this aspect, are these American investments good or bad for Canada? It would seem that Canada stands to gain when the United States erects factories, as these are nationalized behind the tariff wall, and Canadians are employed, or people who eventually become Canadians. Also, such assets cannot be transferred, they can only be left where they are. On the other hand, their control over any source of raw materials whatsoever is bad, because the American capitalist would prefer to extract the riches from the soil in their raw form, and transport them to the United States to be manufactured there. The policy is only too well known in South America where, for a long time now, weak governments have allowed a part of the country's substance to be lost in this way. It is not desirable for Canada that such should be the nature of the American interest in her territory.

We must not overlook the existence of Canadian capital invested abroad. In January 1934 it amounted to $2,028,787,000 of which $1,254,246,000 was in the

U.S.A., $109,997,000 in Great Britain, and $664,544,-000 in other countries. The importance of these figures is that they emphasize the real initiative for foreign investment that exists in Canada. This is particularly manifest in the case of the insurance companies, who accounted for one quarter of the total. Public utilities and other industries were also important. Within the country, however, the interest of the investing public is less adventuresome in the bonds of either the federal or the provincial governments. Nevertheless, although a capacity to accumulate capital undoubtedly exists in times of prosperity, the country still continues to solicit money from abroad, not only American and English, but French and European generally. There is no reason why the reply should not be favourable, for today, when nothing seems secure, Canada may be considered an excellent refuge.

§ 4

By taking these various elements into consideration, we can form a fairly accurate idea of the fundamentals of the Canadian balance of payments.

Let us first look into the debit position. It consists mainly of interest and dividend payments to be made on foreign capital. The Dominion Bureau of Statistics values this item at 219 million dollars for the year 1935. The sum is large enough to class Canada among the borrowing countries along with all the rest of North and South America, except the U.S.A. The second item is freight, estimated at $29 millions. As for the third, which represents the remittances of immigrants to their families who remained in Europe, this must have been very large twenty years ago, when people were coming into the country in their hundreds of thousands, but it is now negligible and does not exceed $700,000. In addition to these three items $15,300,000 must be put down for various foreign payments, making a debit total of $264 millions.

We must now look for the counterpart in a variety of foreign receipts. The most important is the favourable trade balance, when there is one, which is not always the case. In 1935 the favourable margin of exports amounted to $137 millions, and $198 millions if we include the invisibles. Although it attained $401 millions in 1926, and even $623 millions in 1918, there have been many deficits, for example $103 millions in 1930.

A second source of income and equally important is provided by the tourist traffic, which has been greatly increased by the motor car, and by prohibition until it was repealed, and is always favourably influenced by the proximity of the United States. When the season opens, or even when a convention is held in one of the Canadian towns—what an attraction when the United

States was still dry!—immense hotels, especially equipped for the purpose, fill up with a flood of visitors. The Dominion Bureau of Statistics estimates at $100 millions the net receipts from this source in the year 1935—but this is only the net figure in a mediocre year. The gross amount of money deposited in the country by this rush of people reaches $300 millions, I should imagine, when prosperity is at its height.

If we add the $2,800,000 of sundry receipts from other foreign sources, we reach a credit total of $300,-800,000. Therefore 1935, a year of depression, had a slight credit balance without taking into consideration the export of the gold produced from Canadian mines. In a prosperous year, like 1928 for instance, the favourable balance is large for the interest charges were not more than $166 millions, while the export surplus and tourist traffic brought in respectively $143 millions and $168 millions.

Let us deliberately set to one side the movements of capital, and consider only the factors in this balance of payments which are more or less stable. Although we cannot generalize on the figures during a depression, the year 1935 will suit our purpose well enough, especially if we are careful to remember that the prosperous years from 1924 to 1929 were also representative of Canada's development. Thus in a favourable period, when export trade is active and tourists numerous and full of money, Canada easily finds the means to meet and even exceed the charges on her external debt. She then has a credit balance, as was the case during the war and in the boom after the war, and even surplus capital to invest. But in times of depression, the burden of the interest which must be sent abroad weighs heavily on her, and as soon as exports and tourists languish, accounts will not balance and the situation is reversed.

From these facts we conclude that Canada ought always to have a favourable trade balance. This rule is common to her and all other borrowing countries, notably all American countries with the exception of the United States, and even the latter was in this category up to the time of the war. All this is perfectly natural. Long before the war came to remind us conclusively, political economy taught us that debts are paid for in merchandise, and that a debtor economy—assuming that it intends to honour its engagements—must always have a favourable balance of trade.

This is why Canada, and it cannot be repeated too often, is obliged to export. It is her method of paying her debts, and she has no alternative. Payment is made differently according to whether the debt is English or American. In the first case it is made by exporting raw materials, wheat being the most important factor in the operation. In the second case invisible exports representing the tourist traffic are added to exports of real

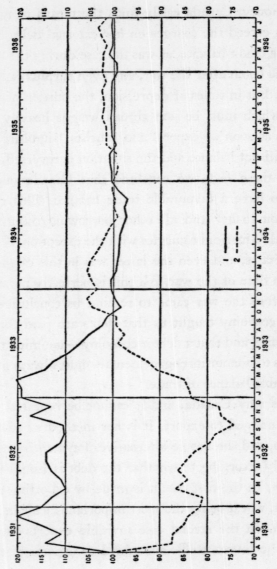

MONTREAL QUOTATIONS IN CANADIAN DOLLARS OF THE AMERICAN DOLLAR AND THE POUND STERLING

1. American Dollar   2. Pound Sterling

merchandise—newsprint and farm produce. If we add together both visible and invisible items we must conclude that, in spite of the customs figures, it is the United States and not England who is Canada's best customer, as well as her main source of supply.

The monetary problem is based on the foregoing arguments. The Canadian currency is the dollar, or at least the Canadian dollar, and it is with the American dollar that it is really linked. Everything militates in this direction—the proximity of the two countries, and the fact that the Stock Exchange is open during the same hours in Montreal and New York, whereas the afternoon is already half over in London when offices open in Montreal. Also Canadian and American financiers have the same way of working, they breathe the same atmosphere, and are brought extraordinarily close together by similarity of habits and interests. Nevertheless, Canada cannot disinterest herself from the pound sterling, and because of this her dollar is not an integral part of the American currency.

Its intermediary position between the pound and the American dollar is the result of the balance of transactions between the three countries. When she exports wheat to the British market, Canada is paid in sterling, which she then sells in New York to pay for her imports from the United States. Under such conditions it is to her interest that the pound should be strong and the dollar relatively weak, for she buys in the United States all her industrial equipment, which is North American in character. A state of equilibrium is thus established by a triangular interplay. It automatically corrects the constantly recurring tendency to get out of adjustment. Certain export interests prefer the Canadian dollar to decline in relation to the pound, in order to stimulate their sales of wheat. On the other hand, because they are in debt to the United States, the Canadians may wish to see the American dollar weaken in order to make their payments more easily. Also in such an eventuality would not American possessors of Canadian bonds sell them to profit by the situation?

Owing to the play of these and a hundred other compensations, a level tends to be spontaneously established. It is the result of laws as natural as those of hydrostatics. Therefore when the pound and the American dollar diverge, the Canadian dollar remains steady about half-way between them, to rally to their common level when they return to normal. For example, when the pound sterling declined after September 1931, the Canadian dollar increased its value in sterling, but declined in American currency. In December 1931 the pound was worth in Montreal only $3.76⅜ against $4.87⅜ at the end of August, while the American dollar advanced from $1.00⅟₁₆ to $1.13⅟₁₆. This signifies that the Canadian dollar had not depreciated as much as the pound, but also that it had not remained as high as the American dollar. When, after April 1933, the American dollar was depreciated in its turn, what do we find? The Canadian dollar depreciated in relation to the pound, and increased in relation to the American dollar. The pound was quoted once more in Montreal in September 1933 at $4.85, but the American dollar had declined to $1.02³⁄₁₆, which signifies that, each of the two currencies having declined in its turn, Canada had adjusted herself more or less to the same proportions as before the crisis.

The ideal condition for Canada is certainly that there be a fixed relationship between the American dollar and the pound sterling, and similarly, on the political horizon, no cloud to mar the friendship between Washington and London.

IV

THE POLITICAL ASPECT

CHAPTER XI

CANADA'S INTERNATIONAL STATUS

§ I

CANADA's political problem results from a duality of allegiances both of which seem to be an innate part of her destiny. Although geographically American, Canada is, at the same time, the one big country in the New World belonging to a non-American empire. Although autonomous within the British community, she is not completely independent. Nor is she united, for the French are still a distinct element, and the immigrants of cosmopolitan origin become Canadians when they are assimilated, without ever having been English. In the end everybody will probably be Americanized. Economically we have seen that serious conflicting interests exist between the various regions. The industrial East is opposed to the agricultural West; British Columbia has little in common with the older provinces on the Atlantic. As the country stretches out in a ribbon extending indefinitely from east to west, these contrasts exert a centrifugal action which may eventually become dangerous.

There is, however, a desire for union which has prevailed up to the present time, under all circumstances and in spite of many temptations. Three-quarters of a century ago, the British faced the future of Canada with singularly little optimism. Their experience of American secession, still comparatively recent, seemed to presage a similar separation. Canada would be absorbed by the United States, or possibly, according to a favourite formula, would break away peacefully "as ripe fruit falls from the tree." Yet her evolution has been quite different, for although independence has been realized, it has not been accompanied by separation in any form. This is so unprecedented that it awakens the admiration of all thinkers, who marvel at such wisdom. And yet no definite solution appears to have been reached, though perhaps, as the sage has said, there never is a solution to anything. So the future remains uncertain.

We must tread warily through this tangle, for we cannot ignore it if we wish to determine the fundamentals of Canadian policy. In marshalling these problems —rather arbitrarily perhaps—we shall first see how Canada attained to international status; then, within the political sphere of the country itself, we shall consider the position taken up, first by the English and then by the French Canadian element, not forgetting the dominating influence of their American neighbour. Only then will the foreign policy of the Dominion be clear. If we wish to extend the scope of the discussion, we can then examine the country's international position, in the political and economic equilibrium of the twentieth century, which is the real subject of this work.

§ 2

"Geographically, and also historically, one can distinguish three British Empires." This significant remark was made by Sir Alfred Zimmern, professor at Oxford. From the point of view of geography, the first group consisted of the settlement colonies, which became the Dominions; the second was made up of the exploitation colonies, corresponding more or less to the Crown Colonies; and finally the scattered group of naval bases and oil and coal stations. Similarly, from the historical approach, it is easy to trace three chapters in imperial history: first, the Empire of the Colonial Pact, based upon force and the mercantile theory. This empire died from too much restraint in 1783 with the loss of the United States. Second, that of colonial autonomy and economic liberty, victoriously carried on throughout the nineteenth century and terminated less by coming to an end than by expansion into the third. This was the Commonwealth, founded on the independence and equality of the Dominions. It is more than an empire, being in reality a federation of nations. The constitutional development of Canada should be studied in conjunction with this imperial evolution. We must carefully note the extra-American character of Canadian policy.

In the second half of the nineteenth century, as part of the liberal policy inaugurated about 1840, England set up a form of empire, which was based on the autonomy of the settlement colonies. The mother country maintained a high-handed control over general policy, as was her sovereign right. Thus imperial unity was fully safeguarded. Under this regime, which was prolonged into the opening year of the twentieth century, and which I personally saw in actual practice, Canada was satisfied with the right to manage her own internal affairs as she pleased. She did not appear to be anxious to influence British foreign policy, nor even to have her own sovereignty recognized to any degree. She was engrossed in the problems of her continental development, and therefore, provided their interests were not neglected nor sacrificed by Downing Street, the Ottawa Governments congratulated themselves on leaving London to carry out on their behalf a host of international negotiations which were both costly and difficult.

Canada did not object to this dependence on the metropolis. It was from England, the sovereign state, that the Dominion derived the power to make her own laws, a power which had been granted to her and theoretically could be withdrawn. This dependence was manifested in the presence of a Governor-General, uniting in his person two distinct functions. In internal matters he was an impartial arbiter, and, like the King, whose lieutenant he was, he could not be held responsible; but he became a British agent once more whenever the question at issue went beyond the colonial sphere. Fortified with instructions, verbal at any rate, he was chiefly concerned with maintaining Canadian policy in harmony with that of the Empire. Had he not shown consummate tact, the figure of the proconsul might have emerged from behind that of the viceroy.

But the principle of autonomy, which had lain in the minds of the colonials since the time of Durham and Elgin, was eventually bound to develop to its logical sequence. England applied the brakes, less by her statesmen, who were being steadily won over to the Liberal conception, than by her civil servants who were slower to change. At each demand from the colonies, the Colonial Office declared that that was the end of the Empire. . . . And yet the logic of the situation always won out in the end. Canada thus obtained the right to set up her own tariff, to control her own budget, to govern herself freely, and to lead her own life without outside interference. Little by little the Governors-

General ceased to exert the rights which they retained in theory. "Do what you are told," became the essence of their instructions. This regime, in which precedents were imperceptibly transforming themselves into rights by a sort of acquisitive prescription, already contained the seeds of independence.

Very soon, as it happened, the domain of strict autonomy no longer sufficed. Once the Canadian Government had been authorized to set up its own tariff, was it likely to abstain from discussing its fiscal relations with foreign countries? But here, barring the road, rose up the fiction of British sovereignty, in virtue of which all separate negotiations seemed to mean a claim to independence. The British Government found a compromise which, for several generations, seemed to be sufficient. The colonies did not receive the right to make treaties, but they were allowed to conduct their own commercial negotiations. The British ambassador presented the colonial representative, as a matter of form, to the foreign government; then he retired, to appear again only at the last moment, when, with great formality, he appended his signature to a diplomatic document in which he had scarcely collaborated. The real negotiator, by courtesy, was also asked to sign, but in the midst of so much diplomatic pomp, he suddenly rebecame a very humble figure indeed, lost in the majesty

of the British Empire. Though it flattered the snobbishness of some colonials, to others such diplomatic haught-
iness was very distasteful. Nevertheless this *modus
vivendi*, which expressed the English genius for compromise to perfection, worked marvellously. The signature of Great Britain, symbol of sovereignty, saved
everyone's face. One may argue that England was re-
leasing the substance to chase the shadow, but this very
shadow had the real prestige value. This was especially
so since, in this purely formal tutelage, there was sometimes the possibility of intervening behind the scenes.
The protocol, this ritual of policy, thus became a bulwark of imperial unity.

Under such a regime which, almost until yesterday
was the imperial scheme, the metropolis conceded almost everything, and yet officially kept everything intact. To say that all Canadians were pleased with this
solution would be going too far. They realized its advantages, but the feeling was growing that their independence should be recognized. Sir John Macdonald
was aware of this national consciousness, and Sir Wilfrid
Laurier reflected it when, early in the twentieth century, he proudly proclaimed, almost as part of his platform, "Canada is a nation!" But with this idea new
demands were voiced, which the preceding generations
had never thought of. Hitherto they had been content

with semi-independence, in practice even though not by right, but in future they would not be satisfied with anything less than outright recognition.

They lost patience with the outworn English conceit (apparently it existed within the Empire as well as elsewhere!) of regarding "colonials" (a slightly disdainful term) as second-rate Englishmen. The tone of the Colonial Office, which thought it was still administering Canada's affairs fifty years after independence had been granted, irritated Canadians to exasperation. Finally, the secrecy of the Foreign Office, which carried on imperial policy without consulting them, began to shock them as an anachronism. It was clearly apparent by about 1910 that the traditional *modus vivendi* of the nineteenth century was no longer in keeping with the aspirations of a colony, which rejected the term as beneath its dignity.

A school of thought, which was growing in numbers under the brilliant inspiration of John S. Ewart, author of the *Kingdom Papers*, and to which Laurier certainly rallied after his fall from power in 1911, defined the limits of the political bond with England as a simple union through having the same sovereign. This great prime minister did not wait until he had gone into opposition to claim explicitly on behalf of Canada the right to possess her own diplomatic corps.

A superficial observer would almost be justified in jumping to the conclusion that the imperial ties were seriously weakening, but he would be mistaken. Coinciding with their desire for a recognition of independence, there was also a growing sentiment among Canadians in favour of the Empire and its unity. In truth they may have feared imperial centralization, but they had no wish for separation, for after 1890 the idea of American annexation went out of date. On the contrary, they were proud of belonging to the Empire, and eager to give tangible proof of their devotion. The preferential tariff in 1897, and the Canadian participation in the South African War were turning points.

England's great wisdom at this juncture was that she realized that, although apparently contradictory, the two tendencies of colonial opinion could be combined to strengthen the Empire, though not without transforming it. By a happy chance a new imperialist school which took this spirit into account was formed in England at about this time. Chamberlain's imperialism, in spite of his sincere respect for colonial autonomy, nevertheless involved a tendency towards centralization which would have stood in the way of the inevitable evolution of Canada's colonial personality. In a sense he went beyond Gladstonian Liberalism, which he had ceased to represent, for he aimed at rejuvenating certain characteristics of the Colonial Pact, and renewing the tradition of this "first Empire," which had disappeared with so little regret. But under the influence of Cecil Rhodes, of Lord Milner, and later of the militant apostles of the "Round Table," a new doctrine emerged after the South African War. It was no longer a question of young British colonies gathering around the metropolis like children at their mother's knee, but a conception of imperial unity which meant complete equality for all its parts.

Henceforth, to borrow a saying from Pascal and apply it to this political constellation, the Empire should be like "a sphere in which the centre is everywhere and the circumference nowhere." Unity of sentiment between the members was to be the true and essential tie. "I believe," Rhodes had declared as early as 1883, "that each colony, on which self-government is conferred, should constitute practically an independent republic. . . . But I also believe," he added, "that the colonials should avail themselves of all the privileges which are provided for them by the tie which binds them to the Empire."

Such formulae, whether he knew it or not, expressed to the letter the aspirations of a Canada arriving at political maturity, and wishing, without leaving the Empire, to affirm her unrestricted independence. They also corresponded to the outlook which predominated more and more in the English governing class on the eve of the war. At the Imperial Conference of 1911, it is significant to find Sir Edward Grey for the first time taking the assembled prime ministers into his confidence in matters of foreign policy. Already we have the atmosphere of collaboration between equals which was to be the rule in the Empire during the Great War. This was the embryo of the "third British Empire."

The war naturally developed aspirations that had previously been vague and inarticulate. After their magnificent co-operation in the heroic struggle England could no longer treat the Dominions as her wards to be inspired and directed. The English people, however, did not all see matters in this light. The Canadian officers often complained that they were not treated by British officers with the consideration which is reserved for social equals—again the same error, the same lack of understanding that the Colonial Office had shown fifty years earlier! An entirely different attitude was shown by the statesmen, who collaborated with the ministers from the Dominions on equal terms.

The Imperial War Cabinet, which sat in London and arose owing to exceptional circumstances, united the members of the British War Cabinet and the colonial prime ministers into a supreme executive council. For this reason, the theory and practice of the Imperial Constitution—if we may thus refer to a group of institutions which prefer deliberately not to be formulated—evolved more quickly than they would have in normal times. After the Imperial War Conference of 1917, a vitally important meeting because of the orientation of policy which it decided, it was recognized unreservedly that the Dominions should henceforth be considered as fully grown nations, and that they were justified in possessing, even in the conduct of foreign affairs, their own point of view corresponding to their special interests. At the same time it was declared, emphatically and by common agreement, that this proclaimed independence in no way threatened the solidity of the imperial tie.

In a speech delivered at the conference on April 16th, 1917, Sir Robert Borden, Prime Minister of Canada, said, "The policy of according absolute control in our domestic affairs and complete autonomy in our local administration, far from having slackened the ties which unite us to the Empire, has, on the contrary, greatly strengthened them."

The ninth resolution of the conference contained a formula which is essential both in its novelty and in its import. It stated that all future revision of imperial status should be based upon the full recognition of the

Dominions, as autonomous nations of an Imperial Commonwealth.[1]

The Dominions, as we have shown, have enjoyed since before the war actual independence that was almost complete. The new factor is that they are agreed that henceforth this independence shall be fully recognized, even by foreigners—in other words, that they shall be given an international status. It was in this spirit that they obtained the right to affix their signatures to the Treaty of Versailles, following but alongside that of Great Britain, and then to a separate vote in the League of Nations, of which they are members through being part of the British Empire, but where they also figure as political entities on their own account.

[1] Ninth Resolution of the Imperial War Conference of 1917.

IX

CONSTITUTION OF THE EMPIRE

THE Imperial War Conference are of opinion that the readjustment of the constitutional relations of the component parts of the Empire is too important and intricate a subject to be dealt with during the War and that it should form the subject of a special Imperial Conference to be summoned as soon as possible after the cessation of hostilities.

They deem it their duty, however, to place on record their view that any such readjustment, while thoroughly preserving all existing powers of self-government and complete control of domestic affairs, should be based upon a full recognition of the Dominions as autonomous nations of an Imperial Commonwealth, and of India as an important portion of the same, should recognize the right of the Dominions and India to an adequate voice in Foreign Policy and in Foreign Relations, and should provide effective arrangements for continuous consultation in all important matters of common Imperial concern, and for such necessary concerted action, founded on consultation, as the several Governments may determine.

From this moment and for this reason a new conception of the Empire took the place of the one that had
prevailed since the middle of the nineteenth century.
There was no longer a sovereign mother country surrounded by colonies, autonomous and deferential, nor
yet a unified empire, with, as its executive, a cabinet
which was at once imperial and British. Henceforth,
according to the terms adopted by the Imperial Conference of 1926—which in reality only confirmed what
was already in existence—"Great Britain and the Dominions are within the Empire autonomous collectivi-
ties of equal status; they are in no way subordinate one
to the other, and from no point of view, domestic or
foreign; but they are united by a common allegiance
to the same crown, and freely associated as members
of the community of British nations."

Commenting upon this vital clause, the Hon. Ernest
Lapointe, a Canadian cabinet minister, adds a definition
which is scarcely less important: "This declaration, this
affirmation of the status of the British nations, is not a
unilateral article emanating from Great Britain, nor
from any one part of what is commonly called the British Empire; it is not a charter granted by a superior
power to subordinate territories. It is a recognition, by
equals and associates, of a condition accepted by all." [1]

[1] The Hon. Ernest Lapointe, "Le Statut International du Canada,"
Revue Trimestrielle Canadienne, December 1927.

The British genius, thanks to its traditional supple-
ness, thus created—or allowed to be created—a new
type of political community, of which history affords
no other example. We have just enumerated its basic
principles, but the Statute of Westminster (1931) man-
aged, almost, to deprive these principles of all the logic
they contained. No act of the British Parliament can
in future apply to the Dominions except at their request. The Colonial Validity Act of 1866 annulled completely all colonial legislation which was contrary to
British legislation, but this provision now ceases to exist.
As the Imperial Conferences of 1929 and 1930 have
abolished any veto from London on laws enacted by
the Dominions, it follows that the British parliament
now legislates only for territory which is strictly under
its control, namely the United Kingdom and the Crown
Colonies. This theory has not been carried out to its
logical conclusion, however. For the constitutions which
created the Canadian Confederation in 1867, and the
Australian Commonwealth in 1901, were the result in
each case of a vote in the British parliament and can
only be amended by a similar vote. Now, at the express
desire of the interested parties themselves, it continues
to be the case until further notice. This reserve, to which
we shall return presently, will allow us to glance at certain contradictions in the Canadian personality.

In spite of this hitch in the harmony of the system,

the fact remains that, without undue haste, but with a will that has never deviated no matter which party was in power, Canada has assured herself of all the organs of sovereignty. Although Australia made much more stir about it during the war, she follows a long way after, and for reasons which we appreciate. Ireland must obviously be classed apart. In the transformed Empire it is Canada that represents, even more than the Union of South Africa, the type of Dominion which has evolved towards independence. We must study this new order of things under its principal aspects, and especially in so far as it modifies Canada's relations with either her old metropolis or with foreign powers.

§ 3

So far as Canada's relations with England are concerned, it is admitted that in future there will exist between the two countries only the bonds of a personal union under the same sovereign—the Imperial Conference of 1926 and the Statute of Westminster left no doubt on this point. If anything to the contrary still remains in the statutes, such as for example the necessity of intervention by the British Parliament in the case of any revision of the British North America Act of 1867, or the appeal to the Privy Council, we must see in them only verbal survivals destined to disappear, unless it be that many Canadians continue to regard arbitration by an older, impartial and distant body as a valuable guarantee. But, having made this reservation, all trace of subordination is henceforth wiped out, and we are in the presence of two states of equal status. Although adhered to by custom, the terms Imperial Parliament and Imperial Government no longer, juridically, mean anything in so far as the Dominions are concerned.

The significance of the Crown itself has also changed. For the English it is indivisible, but the Canadians are also pleased to consider that the King of England is also King of Canada, or at least, and not without a touch of subtlety, King in Canada. Actually, it was as King of Canada, supported only by his Canadian ministers, that Edward VIII took part in the Vimy celebrations in July, 1936.

It would, after all, be logical for the Dominion to have a flag of its own, but this we must confess is a difficult problem—all plans so far having required at least ten pages of explanations and reservations. Meanwhile it is the Union Jack that one sees everywhere, though with the tricolour where there are French Canadians. The Governor-General hoists a special flag of his own, not the Union Jack, thereby emphasizing a territorial separation which must not be overlooked. Under these conditions the Governor-General as Viceroy continues to be as before the representative of the

Crown; but it is simply this and no more, as there can be no further question of his being considered as a British agent. In virtue of a custom which seems likely to continue, his choice is suggested to the King by the Canadian Government itself, without the English Cabinet having anything to say. He might not be an Englishman—there is nothing to prevent it.

The Conservatives in Canada seem to prefer an outstanding member of the aristocracy who is imbued with etiquette, but the Liberals are attracted rather to an outstanding civil servant, or someone with intellectual prestige. We must not think that because he no longer receives instructions from the metropolis, that the Viceroy's duties are merely decorative. It is certainly understood that he shall not interfere—he would not be forgiven if he did—but, like a Prince Consort, he can exert a great deal of influence. The policy of a great Viceroy may have lasting consequences. He is an example, a living symbol of good form, in a continent where it is tempting to lapse into easy democratic manners; he inspires and even creates institutions which survive him; and in cultural matters he interprets Canada to herself. Finally, by his mere presence, he maintains the link with Great Britain.

On the other hand, the function of being a direct political liaison is outside his province. He is no longer the channel of official communication between London and Ottawa. At the time of the war the practice arose of British and Dominion Prime Ministers corresponding directly, a copy of the proceedings "for information" being handed to the Governor-General. But even the copy is now dispensed with, since he is no longer in any sense an intermediary channel. A succession of diplomatic substitutes have been set up to replace this out-of-date machinery. For many years Canada has had her own High Commissioner in London, and the British Government has now nominated one in its turn at Ottawa. For the latter post they must avoid appointing a man who is too much of a diplomat, as his attitude might suggest a foreign ambassador; nor yet too much of a political personality, whom the Canadians might suspect of wishing to intrude in their affairs. Up to the present the choice has been made among highly placed civil servants with technical experience. With tact they have moved in diplomatic circles as if they were not part of the family—it is sometimes said that the American minister seems to be more at home! The whole business is very clever. Thus a rejuvenated political bond is being reconstructed, and seems to be functioning with complete efficiency.

From this survey we see that the Imperial Conference of 1926 only confirmed practices which had been in existence ever since the war. Yet it is easy to understand that the old British tutelage in official matters cannot long survive the birth of this new spirit. Not that the Canadians asked for any new powers with regard to negotiations, but simply that they were beginning to tire of the symbolic intervention, even though it were discreet, of a permanent diplomatic *chaperon*. Back in the days of the Laurier Government, a department of foreign affairs was created at Ottawa. A time came, however, shortly after the Treaty of Versailles, when the Canadian Government went a step farther, and insisted that its treaties should bear only its own signature.

The conflict over procedure between London and Ottawa in February and March 1923 marked a decisive point in the evolution of Canada's diplomatic status. It was a question of a treaty concerning the halibut fisheries in the north Pacific Ocean. It had been negotiated directly, as was customary, between the governments at Washington and Ottawa. When it was finally concluded, the British Ambassador to the United States was prepared as usual for a joint signature, British and Canadian, with the British signing first of course. But, acting on the instructions of the cabinet of which he was a member, the Hon. Ernest Lapointe, Minister of Marine and Fisheries, insisted on signing alone. He kept to his point, and succeeded in making London accept it. Hitherto England had been rigid over matters of procedure, but now for the first time, she gave way.

This event was of great consequence, since after the Imperial Conference of 1923, this practice became the recognized custom. It was admitted from then on, and incidentally confirmed by the Imperial Conference of 1926, that in future all governments in the Empire should have the same right to enter into negotiations, to conclude them, and even to sign treaties with foreign powers in the name of the King. Previously such treaties had been concluded in the name of the British Empire. If it is a question of interests pertaining to Canada only, they will be signed henceforth, naturally in the name of the King, but in respect of the Dominion of Canada. The Canadian plenipotentiary, accredited by the Crown, alone will append his signature. In 1895, in a celebrated dispatch, Lord Ripon, the British Minister for the Colonies, expressed the opinion that granting colonial governments power to negotiate treaties without the assistance of the Empire was not compatible with the maintenance of imperial unity. The future will decide whether he was right.

The power to negotiate and make separate treaties evidently involves the right to create a separate and permanent diplomatic representation, and also the right to receive duly accredited diplomatic agents. Many powers have long had their consuls-general in Canada, but the hostility of the official British attitude has prevented them from carrying out effective diplomatic functions. Prior to the war, with the exception of the Canadian Commissioner-General in Paris, who did not have diplomatic rank, the Canadian Government had not established any permanent representation abroad, not even in Washington where negotiations over Canadian affairs are almost a daily occurrence. At the conclusion of peace, owing to the new international status being recognized, it was quite natural that the Ottawa Government should consider creating a permanent and special representation in the American capital. England acquiesced, though not without reserves and reluctance. London suggested a Canadian Minister Plenipotentiary who would be an adjunct to the British Ambassador, a collaborator and member of a sort of imperial embassy, who would remain as chargé d'affaires in the absence of his chief. Another plan—to save face as usual—was to appoint a Canadian as British Ambassador to the United States. Whatever the form, it was bound to be rather a delicate role to fill, and no doubt it was for this reason that the project, though contemplated ever since 1920, was not carried out until 1926. But considerable water has flowed under the bridge, and while they were trying to make up their minds the question came to fruition. Mr. Vincent Massey, the first Canadian Minister Plenipotentiary appointed to Washington, was established there, not as an adjunct to the British Ambassador, but with his own offices, and with complete independence of action. Since then the combination has functioned without friction, thanks to the perfect loyalty of the English, and this time it is the Canadians who seem perfectly at home on the banks of the Potomac.

It was not surprising that in 1928, by agreement with the powers interested, the Canadian Government proceeded to create two new legations, one in Tokio and the other in Paris, while France decided to transform her consulate-general in Canada into a legation. The new minister was none other than our old friend M. Phillippe Roy, former Commissioner-General, who under various titles has represented his country in France for twenty years. He was then accredited to the President of the Republic, who previously had not been authorized by a jealous officialdom to recognize him. As Ottawa was now receiving various foreign ministers, the Canadian capital for the first time became a diplomatic centre, elevating itself in keeping with its new international status.

§ 4

The future will disclose whether the Empire comes out of this evolution with greater strength than before. For what may prove to be a long phase, it will assuredly tap new sources of life and moral strength. But exactly how much remains of imperial unity?

The Crown is the essential, the unique symbol, supported by certain prerogatives whose prestige should not be despised, even in America. The right of pardon, of conferring honours, of the usage of the seal, and of the Royal procedure has been strictly preserved for the Viceroy. The Dominion Government having first demanded and then obtained all sovereign rights, the only constitutional link now existing between the various parts of the Empire is a personal union. The exception is the appeal to the Privy Council in civil matters—criminal appeal to Westminster has not existed in Canada since 1888. And the right of appeal, while it lasts, is a survival of actual union. But is the fiction of Royal unity sufficient to compensate for the factors of dissociation which are growing with increasing force?

In truth, the circumstances in which Empire unity can be translated into common political action are becoming increasingly rare. In the immediate past the direction of foreign affairs, British or imperial, were one and the same, and remained by common accord the exclusive domain of the Foreign Office. Today the right to formulate a general policy for the Empire belongs only to the peoples who compose it—when they are represented at the Imperial Conferences. Their agreement can create a policy, but any member that declines to be a party to it can keep his international liberty. In the intervals between these sessions, while no permanent organ of the Conference exists, without doubt the Foreign Office is in fact and by tacit consent charged with any decision and its execution when immediate action is necessary. The political leadership of England in the imperial community has thus persisted, up to a certain point, by habit as it were. But as the Dominions become conscious of their international individuality, the old blending of the British and imperial roles will diminish, whereas the diplomatic competence of the former colonies will become more clearly defined in relation to the metropolis. The idea that in future each can have its own foreign policy—a conception formerly considered fatal to the Empire—is now, in spite of certain regrets even in Canada, accepted as perfectly natural.

The Canadian Government, being ahead of the other Dominions in this respect, has evolved a doctrine of perfect clarity. Without denying the solidarity of the Empire, they insist on remaining sole judge of the obligations it involves for them, even in case of war. The old formula that a treaty signed by England is binding upon the Empire, in their opinion, is out of date. They no longer consider themselves bound, except when, having been consulted or solicited, they have expressly given their consent. The new procedure, adopted by the Imperial Conference of 1926, which specifies whether an international engagement has been entered into "on behalf of Great Britain" or "on behalf of the Dominion of Canada," leaves no doubt on this subject. Even since the war this desire for a distinct policy has been affirmed under many different circumstances. In 1922, for example, at the time of the Chanak incident, when, without sufficient preparation, Canada was asked to collaborate in the defence of the Dardanelles, she declined. In 1924 the Canadian Prime Minister declared he did not wish to sign the Treaty of Lausanne, as he had been party neither to its preparation nor its discussion. Again in 1926, England contracted the Locarno Treaty alone without obtaining the support of the Canadian signature.

The attitude is always clear and always the same. Canada commits herself when her interests are involved, but she no longer considers herself as part of a whole, but as a distinct and independent personality. Therefore, alongside English policy, there is a special Canadian policy, which must be taken into account. Under these conditions the term Empire, in the Roman sense, no longer applies to the British system throughout the world. The term Commonwealth, which is gradually replacing it, corresponds to a different conception. The individuality of the parts will in the end do away with the whole, to a certain extent. "The Empire," a Canadian humorist said to me, "is like a giraffe, of which one sees only the spots. The spots are the Dominions, but as for the giraffe, well, there ain't no such animal!"

We seem to be getting back to the old medieval discussion of realism and nominalism. So far as I personally am concerned, I cannot help believing that the unity of the Empire does exist, but less in the form of a state than as a community of political conceptions extending to all British peoples and comprehensible more or less to all Anglo-Saxons. There is nothing in the existence of such a group contrary to the independence of its component parts.

CHAPTER XII

BRITISH INFLUENCE

At first view the impressions one obtained of the English Canadians is clearly defined, but on closer acquaintance subtle distinctions arise, and the fine simplicity vanishes. There is the Englishman, born in England, who has recently migrated to Canada, and who is still intensely English. There is his son who is being brought up in Canada in an atmosphere of loyalty to Britain, and who seems to be part of a British garrison. Then there is the Canadian of British origin, still mindful of this fact, although he has become assimilated to American surroundings. Alongside him is the English-speaking Canadian, whose family arrived so long ago that he is out of touch with the Old Country. In each of these types one must sort out the English from the Scots and the Irish, not forgetting the descendants of the United Empire Loyalists, whose ancestors were American for several generations even before they were Canadian. To these we must add a medley of others of foreign origin who also speak English. The gradations of the political tints in these different groups are as delicate as the colours on an artist's palette.

One may say that the Englishman in Canada is English before he is Canadian; to tell the truth he has never ceased to be English and would be surprised if anyone took him for anything else. His allegiance, in so far as British nationalism has a territorial allegiance, lies outside the country; politically his heart is far away, somewhere in the northwest of Europe in some corner of the British Isles. It is not he who favours any display of independence, any creation of a separate diplomacy, or any obtaining of the right to sign treaties. On the contrary he regrets these things, and sadly disclaims any innovations which sap imperial unity. At heart, though he does not always admit it, he has a "colonial" mentality. Apart from the liberties which he prizes like the rest of his compatriots, he has no wish for a new nationality, which to him could not replace the elementary pride in being English. In case of war he would react immediately as a "Britisher," and would rush to the flag—to the British flag. We all know English people of this type, for they are the same the world over.

The attitude of the English Canadian is different, for he is first of all a Canadian, and feels that he is distinct from the English. We must admit that he does not like them, and is always running them down. They are, he says, proud, disdainful, intimidating and incomprehensible. They are not good mixers, they do not become assimilated, and they are not the right "temperature." In short, these brothers are strangers to each other, and the English Canadian is much more at ease with the Americans. But we must be careful here—this Canadian who does not like the English loves England, and, moreover, he clings to the British tie, to the British connection. In his case this sentiment has nothing incompatible with his Canadian independence. The laws which hold a family together are mysterious. One can love one's family, even be devoted to it, without liking every one of its members! The chilliness which one often notices between Canadians and English when they meet—and of which, it seems, there was more than one example at the Ottawa Conference in 1932—has no political repercussions, just as, on the other hand, there are none resulting from the obvious personal sympathy which brings Americans and Canadians together.

England and the Empire can thus count on the support of the English Canadians, always allowing for the fact that the Dominion comes first. Thus their devotion to the Empire, real as it is, is a function of their interest in Canada. But between this attitude and the one indicated above, there are an infinite number of gradations. Thus if England herself were to go to war, it would be difficult to say how far the spontaneous reaction would be English, or Canadian, or Imperial. What we do know is that in matters of secondary importance Canadians are inclined to regard British Imperialism with a certain amount of suspicion. But if the mother country were in mortal danger, filial sentiments would appear even in circles where they are supposed to be out of date.

Having arrived at this point, if we are asked how far Canada is still British, we shall have to answer in a canny Norman fashion, and say that for a year when apples are plentiful their apples are not up to much, but that for a bad apple year then theirs are all right! In transposing this precious fromula, the *chef-d'œuvre* of a peasant wisdom, we should suggest that for an American country the Dominion is English, and for an English country it is American. According to whether one arrives in Canada from the United States or from England, one or other of these two impressions is invariably received. We may say that Americanism in Canada is aggressive and glaring, while British influence is subtle and not immediately apparent, but such judgments must be carefully weighed. Elsewhere in the Empire, countries such as Australia and New Zealand are quite differently tinted with English influence, but when one considers that Canada shares a boundary of 3000 miles with the United States, is it not rather wonderful that a British North America should exist at all?

From the point of culture and civilization, British influence is certainly present, but it is weak. The atmosphere definitely is American, but there is nothing to be done about it, and never will be. Apart from a few limited circles, which are inspired quite as much by snobbishness as by their loyalty to England, Canadians speak very differently from English people. In Australia the national accent is Cockney, but here it is Yankee. When I had been in Canada several months, I was surprised to find that even I instinctively felt that an "Oxford accent" was a pose. "Why can't he talk like everyone else?" was the comment, obscurely suggesting the instinct for equality which dominates the New World. Now this aggressive representative of a linguistic aristocracy was simply speaking English, but I must confess that outside of Europe it did sound a bit queer!

It is just the same with sports. The national game is baseball, as in the United States. Colleges which fan the imperial flame extol cricket, but the crowd will have none of it. They want to play the same games as the Americans do. Yet British culture has deposited a vigorous ferment, in Canada especially in education, where English influence is at once noticeable, and Scottish even more strongly. One cannot say, however, that the intellectual life of the country depends largely on England. A glance at the map convinces us that 130 million inhabitants who are near at hand are more likely to be taken as models than 40 millions who are far off.

Having made these important observations, we are apt to forget the rest. We may say that Canadian institutions are deeply imbued with British inspiration, which holds its own even in spite of geography, and therefore the Dominion occupies a place apart in the American continent. A real frontier separates Canadian institutions from those of the United States. The list may be long, but it is so significant that we shall enumerate it.

Let us begin with the parliamentary spirit. The American continent, which in constitutional matters invented the president, adheres to the tradition of the tribune or plebiscite, and not to that of governments responsible to the assembly. This observation applies not only to the United States, but also to the Latin countries of the New World, where ministers are simply the deputies of all-powerful presidents of the republics. Canada, however, is attached to an entirely different system, to that of a cabinet which is responsible to a parliamentary majority. The political life of Ottawa is American in many ways, but its atmosphere is still remarkably English. There is no President of the Republic—no Republic of any sort—no Congress, but instead there are a Viceroy, a Prime Minister, a House of Commons, in fact a whole procedure inspired by Westminster. A Lincoln, a McKinley, and a Wilson are authentic products of the new continent, but one has the impression that a Sir John A. Macdonald and a Sir Wilfrid Laurier, and a Sir Robert Borden more readily take as their models great English parliamentarians such as Disraeli, Gladstone, and Asquith. These Canadian statesmen are very American if you will, yet they form a distinct group in the New World, and when they come to London they are completely carried away by British prestige. It was very much so in the case of Laurier, although he was French Canadian.

In the Canadian legal world the English lesson has also left a lasting impression. Justice, in this country of liberalism, has been able to preserve its impartiality and moral authority. When Canadians are asked what they consider is the chief difference between the Dominion and the neighbouring Republic they will usually say that it is the way justice is administered, and the Americans agree with them. In this matter the current from the east was able to retain its essential vigour, to the undoubted advantage of the community. The Canadian professions are similarly organized. They are grouped into corporations under royal patronage the same as in England, and this again constitutes a solid link in the relations between the Dominion and the Mother Country—one to which we do not generally attribute sufficient importance. This provides a social structure which is both efficient and stable in comparison with other American countries, which obviously suffer from the lack of it.

As we have already said, the Anglican Church is essentially British in its outlook. Indeed this link with the Empire is so apparent that the Established Church in England has never seriously thought of separation. Along with ecclesiastical ritual must also be classed English procedure, which still persists on all official occasions in Canada. The opening of Parliament by the Governor-General, the receptions at his official residence, Rideau Hall, and the levees which he holds when he is on tour throughout the country, are all further examples of British influence, and are likely to impress an observer with the extent to which they are non-American. What a contrast between an audience with the President of the Republic at the White House, and one with the Governor-General at Ottawa! The personal courtesy and the gracious welcome are the same, but in the second case there is an aloofness that is intended really to indicate the inaccessibility of royal majesty. Such official procedure would be impossible in the United States since the American Revolution, but it is still respectfully accepted in Canada. The public regard it as a reminder, as a lesson in good form, which does not endanger their liberty and prevents in some measure the standard of courtly manners from declining.

At this point we must touch upon the part played by the Crown, which paradoxically continues to enjoy in this democratic society a feudal element of personal loyalty. It is sometimes said that the King is the crowned president of the imperial republic, but I am inclined to disagree. No doubt Canada behaves like a republic, but the people's attitude towards the sovereign is personal. Their devotion, even affection, also embraces in a more general way the whole of the royal family. The King does not trouble anyone—he is so far away—but they know that he exists and, curiously enough, the recent technical progress in broadcasting has accentuated the personal character of the ties which attach him to his subjects. I was in Canada when King George V broadcast his Jubilee address to his subjects over the radio. The effect was staggering—here indeed we had something which is not American!

British influence is still very real, and is exerted in a number of different ways. In actual practice, for example, it appears as if it has preserved the essentials of its traditional position. The old colonial status has ceased to exist, yet foreign powers, although they may recognize the fact in practice, have not received any official notification. Canadians still remain the subjects of His Britannic Majesty. They continue, though no doubt of their own free will, to rely upon the British consulate in those countries where there is no Canadian diplomatic or consular representative. Their passports are issued by the Canadian Government, but in the name of the King, thus establishing their British nationality.

This British nationality, as we know, embraces each and all of the citizens of the various nations in the Commonwealth, so that, from a foreigner's point of view, British nationality maintains its historic unity. In Canada all official effigies are English—the King and members of the royal family appear on the stamps and on the Federal banknotes. At Ottawa they are working on a combination for a Canadian flag, but as yet they have found nothing suitable. Up to the present the Governor-General has always been an Englishman. I realize that on the reverse side of each one of these various ceremonials, I could find a correction which satisfies Canadian vanity perfectly: the Dominion is independent, Canada is Canadian, the King functions only by means of a signature which he would never refuse to grant— all this is true, and yet, since we are in a British country, we must be careful not to underestimate the significance of recognized ritual. In its form it perpetuates an unbroken tradition which is linked up with a living source.

Useless as it may appear, this structure shelters an English influence which is all the more subtle as it is exerted in secret, silently, leaving no trace. Without appearing to alter anything, England has an incomparable way of imperceptibly directing people, governments, and races to her own ends. We must remember that propaganda (I purposely use this unpleasant expression) if allowed to be seen would immediately pro-

voke an indignant reaction: "The meddlesome in-
truders!" But nothing ever does appear. Here is the
Governor-General with his little court, assisted by a
secretary selected from one of the great families of the
Old Country. Don't you imagine that he contributes
in his own time to the work of consolidating the British
tie? Or again, in the business world, there is a visitor,
someone from the City who has come to have a chat, or
an expert from the Bank of England whose counsel is
sought. He is not hailed with the cordiality extended
to the American brother from across the border, with
whom Canadians get along perfectly because he is so
like themselves—good heavens, no! But do not imagine
that they listen to the Englishman with less attention.
There is something indefinable which protects him, and
lends prestige and confidence to his monosyllabic advice.

Socially, as we have said, this Englishman is a foreigner who lowers the temperature slightly by his mere
passage, but politically he penetrates without difficulty
to the interior of the Temple, even to the Holy of
Holies. Even in the United States we find that the English have the same prodigious capacity for penetrating
right to the place where essential decisions are made.
There, in spite of Irish protestation, "Perfidious
Albion" manages, at the right time and place, to make
her counsels heard. All the more so in Canada, where
every town, in the West as well as in the East, contains

a governing clique of English-speaking people, who are ready to be influenced and keep the liaison intact. London completes this elusive pressure by conferring honours, and throwing open the doors of high society and even the Court to those who are socially ambitious. With a few rare exceptions, experience proves that this power of absorption, of seduction—if I may remove from the word any insulting meaning—is nearly always irresistible.

CHAPTER XIII

THE FRENCH CANADIAN
INFLUENCE

§ 1

THE position of the French Canadians is just as complex as that of the Canadians of British origin. It is determined by many contributing factors: history, race, religion, culture, interests, sentiment, affinities, ill-will, regrets, and future hopes. As we already know, these people are French by race and history, British by allegiance, and American by geography. In order to explain their attitude, we must understand their relationship to France, England, and the United States, as well as to America and Europe considered as continental units. We must further study the French Canadian attitude towards the Canadian confederation, for, after all, they are apt to look upon it as somewhat of an external entity of which they do not form a part.

§ 2

To what extent are the French Canadians French? My personal impression is that they are genuinely French, in their physical traits which distinguish them from the English, and still more so in their bearing, their vivacity, and their ease of speech. Their race is again apparent in their individual gifts of intelligence and expression, which make them, in spite of their peasant qualities, the best barristers, excellent doctors (as even the English realize), brilliant adepts of the liberal professions, and remarkably clever politicians. In a mixed assembly one can pick them out even before they speak, particularly, I think, because they are not phlegmatic. From all these points of view, we in France must voluntarily admit that they are members of our family.

But their immediate resemblance ends here. Living for nearly two centuries under British rule has greatly anglicized them, and they have become so accustomed to it that they do not wish to change. In this respect it is we, the French of France, and not the English, who are foreigners to them. This is particularly striking in parliamentary tradition, where they have accepted and assimilated not only British spirit and methods, but even British formalities. A few of them mingle confidently in our political circles, but they are the exception. Ordinarily they are more at ease in London. Laurier, in his courtesy, was reluctant to give his impression of the French regime, but one soon saw that he reserved his admiration for Westminster. Nor is French influence any more evident when it comes to social customs, which were English in the past but have now become completely Americanized, in so far as dress, furniture, household equipment, and even cooking are concerned. This is not surprising, as these are the conditions which prevail on another continent, whose destiny cannot but be different from ours.

The sentiments of the French Canadians towards France are the result partly of our common origin, and partly of their separation from us. They are proud to claim the honour of belonging to the eternal fellowship of France, and the *tricolore* which floats wherever our language is spoken is the visible sign of their fidelity. The feeling that they are part of the French family is very widespread. Many of them on their first visit to France feel instantly that they are at home in their mother country, and they blossom out with unfeigned delight. Above all, they like our simple manners, and the freedom of our social life. From the moment that they board the liner of the Compagnie Transatlantique, they breathe more freely for having escaped from English aloofness, and the rigidity of a social regime which knows no respite.

But let us not generalize too far. How many others, although retaining their love for France in theory, actually do not succeed in getting accustomed to her! This is because they have become too different, and socially ceased to be French. They suffer, quite wrongly, from an inferiority complex, and are persuaded that the

Parisians will laugh at their accent. Perhaps they do not feel at home until they return to the familiar atmosphere of London. Paris and the French, they have to confess, did not please them!

The position is more serious still when it comes to a question of French politics and the French Government, for here, though it seems banal to mention it, they feel themselves separated for ever from us. They have no regret whatever at having accepted the British regime. There is not, and never has been, any *irredentism* in Canada! We lost contact with them after 1763, and they had every right to feel that the mother country, henceforth unworthy of the name, had abandoned them. Further, the revolution of 1789, by directing France along a path which the old colony loathed, turned out to be an event of even greater magnitude in the history of these relations. The French Canadians are democratic, but in the Anglo-Saxon manner. The French Republic was bound to displease them, partly because they are Catholics and it is laical, but also because they are conservative, sometimes so conservative that they are quite mid-Victorian. In spite of their politeness on the subject, one can hardly say that the Republic of Gambetta, of Ferry, and Clemenceau, has ever succeeded in making itself appreciated in the St. Lawrence Valley—sometimes even the polite formalities were lacking.

I shall never forget the scene just after the war at the residence of the Lieutenant-Governor of the Province of Quebec, who was officially receiving a French mission. After the usual toast to the King, everyone awaited the no less formal toast to the President of the French Republic, but all we heard was the fantastic wording, "à la France eternelle!" The archbishop was present, the officious ones explained. . . .

Such a contrast in political outlook is sufficient to explain why our former compatriots have no wish to return to the fold, but their reluctance is aggravated by the great divergence in the destinies of the two continents. The French Canadians consider themselves among the oldest inhabitants of America, and they feel that their destinies lie in the New World. When they see old Europe plunging into an abyss of quarrels that menace her very existence, they stiffen up with bitter brutality and refuse to be implicated. Thus, as Americans, they deny any close relationship with either France or Europe.

§ 3

The French Canadians accept the British regime because it guarantees them the essentials of religion and language; in other words, it allows them to remain distinct.

The fundamental texts in this connection are the

Treaty of Paris (1763) which formally recognized the right of the defeated to profess their faith and worship freely in conformity with the Roman Church within the limits of British law; later the Quebec Act (1774) which, confirming the earlier religious concessions, admitted the use of the French language in official documents, thus putting the two races on the same footing. These principles have been reaffirmed in all later enactments such as the Constitutional Act of 1791, which created the two Canadas; the Act of Union of 1840 which reunited them; and the British North America Act of 1867, which formed the Confederation. The text of the latter was voted by the British Parliament, and therefore cannot be amended, even today, except by its vote; and let us not forget that the initial guarantee of 1763 was the result of a treaty signed by the English power. The French Canadians, at any rate, do not forget it, for they consider that their rights as a minority derive from this treaty with England. This is the explanation of their loyalty to the British connection, a loyalty of which the sincerity is beyond question. We should specify, however, that this loyalty is addressed to England, but not to a Canada which had no political existence at the time that these engagements were undertaken. If left to herself tomorrow, Canada possibly might not ratify them.

The policy of the leading French Canadian clergy

expresses this attitude very clearly. Instinctively they dislike the English Protestants, fearing the effect on their flock of any contact with them. I once heard a priest declaim from the pulpit in his savoury accent, *"Sachez le frança, mais pour l'angla,* don't learn too much!"

This was just a case of local resistance, but when it is a question of high policy the British regime has no more devoted partisans. It is not so much a matter of the heart as of the head, as Mgr. Plessis showed when he said to the English Governor: "His Majesty has no more devoted subject in this province than I, but my devotion goes only as far as my conscience and no further." As a matter of fact whenever the British connection has been seriously threatened, the co-operation of the French clergy has never been found wanting. In 1775 and 1812 against the American menace, during the Great War, and even at the time of the rebellion of 1837—indeed we may say that ever since 1763 the Church has been an essential factor of British rule in Canada. With its immense moral authority it advises political loyalty to its French-speaking adherents. In exchange it obtains by tacit consent a free hand in a domain which is more or less reserved for it.

The pastoral letter of the Cardinal Archbishop of Quebec, on the occasion of the Jubilee of George V in 1935, marvellously expresses the principles on which this attitude is based. It merits being quoted as an admirable lesson in political wisdom.[1]

It first describes the spirit of co-operation which the Empire has every right, under the circumstances, to expect from the French Canadian clergy: "May we recall that we have needed neither a command nor even the expression of a desire on the part of the civil authorities to realize our duty in this matter." This after all is the doctrine of the Church: "The Holy Scriptures of the Old and New Testaments expressly enjoin us to respect the person of the Sovereign, and to obey his just laws." And such doctrine, it may be useful to remind a conquered race, applies to Canada as to anywhere else: "Do not object that no spiritual attachment exists between us and those who have become our masters through the fortunes of war. This was not chance, for there is only Providence."

The argument, as we indicated earlier, is that the English regime has guaranteed to the French their essential privileges: "For those who calmly review the history of our province during the past two centuries, is not this the place to admit that there is every evidence that a mysterious Providence has enveloped it with tenderness? And, to this end, notwithstanding human

[1] Pastoral letter No. 17 from the very eminent Cardinal Archbishop of Quebec and from our Seigneurs, the Archbishop and Bishops of the Civil Province of Quebec, on the occasion of the Jubilee of His Majesty George V, given at Quebec at the Cardinal's Palace, April 8th, 1935.

views and passions, Providence has caused the sceptre of the Kings of England to protect us with its world-wide prestige, guaranteeing our essential rights, through vicissitudes into which it is not our design to enter here." In point of fact, is the Church not accorded a privileged position in Canada?

"Concerning our religious liberties, for example, it so happens that, by the help of Providence, the Catholic Church is better situated here than in almost any other country in the world. . . . By tacit mutual agreement, and reciprocal esteem, an advantageous relationship has been maintained between the Church and the State. In Canada, and especially in our province, the Church has generally been able to develop in an atmosphere of happy liberty, and her sons have been able to benefit thereby. The civil authorities adopt a respectful attitude towards her, and are not indifferent to her consideration."

This loyalty on the part of the Church, which is based on gratitude, also serves the French Canadian race: "It was due to their appreciation of their pastoral duties, and to their loyalty on the one hand and their tactful firmness on the other, that our venerable predecessors prevailed upon our fathers to adopt the new regime, and twice at least they preserved Canada for Great Britain. . . . Is there an enlightened patriot or loyal Canadian who does not admire the courage and undeviating prudence of these Bishops, these saviours, one may say, of the French race in America after the conquest?"

The destiny of the French Canadians has not fundamentally changed, however, since the Treaty of Paris, and it is still within the British Empire that the possibilities of their development are greatest: "The new political conditions in which Canada finds herself within the Empire should not hinder the free expression of our patriotic sentiments. Far from opposing the development of our culture and the maintenance of our tongue, these conditions may rather open up still wider fields. It remains for us to control events in conformity with the law. The Empire is British; it is established in actual fact that there is no exclusive language, and that the Empire embraces different civilizations. The moment may be perhaps never more propitious for our element, by its activity and importance, to claim its appointed place in the sun, under the regime which Providence in its own way has ordained for us."

This vigorous doctrine is that of leaders who appreciate political necessities, and in human affairs know how to relegate sentiment to the place where it belongs. When the French Canadian politicians reach a certain height in their careers, they logically adopt a similar attitude. Like the Church, they also realize that the English regime has allowed the French race to live, but that left to itself it would run the risk of being absorbed by the United States. They are, therefore, in favour of a policy of collaboration with the English in Canada in matters concerning the Confederation, and with the English in England in imperial affairs. This collaboration, exerted first at Ottawa and later followed up in London, never fails to transform those who practise it. Through personal friendships, they link up with the *élite* in Canada and in England. They submit to the influence and the prestige of the wonderful parliamentary tradition, and receive its honours. Many of them finally became thoroughly British in sentiment, like Laurier, who used to say that he was British to the core. Others, who have confined themselves more closely to their own country, contract at Ottawa a certain loyalty to the Confederation, which some of their followers object to, considering it almost a betrayal.

Nevertheless the mass of the public, and even such local leaders as the lesser clergy and members of parliament, do not allow the arguments of high policy to get the better of their own feelings. In their hearts they know full well that the attitude of their leaders is justified, but in the more limited circle of their own personal activities they see something quite different, namely, the necessity of defending the French Canadian in some obscure corner of the battlefield against the English Canadian, of making no concessions, and of carefully avoiding anything that might resemble a compromise.

They know that a King of England exists to whom they owe, without any passionate devotion, a certain loyalty, but to them "the English" are the English Canadians next door, with whom they have a century-old rivalry. As a whole, and without attempting to analyse, they hate everything that is English. Perhaps they are simply sulking—France is their mother, but England is their stepmother!

§ 4

England has accepted, no doubt with regret, the fact that the French Canadians have remained distinct. They have not been anglicized in the past, nor will they be in the future. It needs little reflection to realize that the United States would not have accorded to the conquered race of 1763 the guarantees which have allowed their church, their schools and their language to survive. The American is an assimilator, and a thorough one at that! He is so convinced of his rights that he is almost childish about it. Annexing Canada to the United States would simply have meant that the French element would have been absorbed.

Now we have not minimized the peril of Americanization, which for the French Canadians is far more serious than anglicization. It is not a political danger, but the risk of being totally engulfed both by a great neighbouring country, and by the atmosphere of the continent in which they live. Still, from the point of view of the American continent, a French Canadian is an American, and therefore we must admit that a certain degree of Americanization was inevitable.

Beyond a certain limit, the French Canadians cannot maintain their integrity. The Church alone realizes this. For more than a century, and not without success, she has been busy keeping her flock within a *cordon sanitaire* in order to prevent them from being contaminated by the English Protestants. She is now faced with a whole conception of life which is incompatible with the morals she is trying to instil. In an address given at Quebec by Cardinal Villeneuve on January 8th, 1934, to the members of the Security Leagues, this point of view was forcibly brought out into the open:

"Actually it is dogmas which are at stake, not mere rules of morality. The world no longer believes in original sin, nor does it accept the theory that this sin has left in us the weakness of the flesh and the rebellion of the flesh to the dictates of reason. It not only legalizes the fire of covetousness, but proclaims that the fire should be stirred up. Once this postulate is admitted, everything else in the customs of today can be explained. They have pushed the disorders of the flesh still farther. They have tried to base it on an imaginary science, whose fragile hypotheses have proved false each in turn. There is nudism, the selection of persons for eugenic breeding, the sterilization of defectives and mentally deficient, onanism, and the practice of contraception. In many countries such matters are placed in the hands of the authorities, and are even included in the legal code under pretext that it is necessary for the progress of the race. The Church will not cease to fight against such falsehoods and such corrupting artifices."

The Cardinal did not mention the United States, but his warning applied literally to the fascinating temptations of that Americanism which optimistically puts its confidence in human energy and almost sanctifies production. This peril, which is becoming more menacing every day, has the effect of reinforcing the devotion of the Church to the British regime, which they regard as a counterweight or sort of insurance. "Better the devil you know than the devil you don't know." So they accept the English as something that they know and can cope with and which is not altogether fatal; and in the end they rely on these same English, for fear of something worse.

§ 5

The external relations of the French Canadians are not limited to France, England, and the United States. Strange as it may seem, a chapter can be written about the relationship which exists within the country between the French and English Canadians just as if these were external relations. It is a *modus vivendi* without cordiality. When one becomes acquainted with both circles, one is astonished to find how widely they are separated. Even in cities of mixed population like Montreal, they do not mingle, but live on the same streets in extraordinary ignorance of each other. A certain professor in the French university admitted that he had never met his opposite number in the English-speaking university, although the latter was a well-known man. A certain member of the English social set did not even know the name of one of the most important French Canadians. Since the French speak English it is not so much the language which separates the two communities as it is the religion, and above all their different outlook on life. The very air they breathe is different, although in both cases their furnishings, taking the term in its wider sense, are uniformly American. I remember having breakfasted with a French Canadian in Montreal and having dined with an English Canadian family in Toronto on the same day. The contrast was quite a shock to my senses. It was like experiencing the different pressures in a diving bell. Involuntarily I thought of the uncompromising formula of Maurice Barrès: "Prayers that do not mingle."

And yet, in spite of their persistent reticence, the *modus vivendi* works well enough, because the two races are obliged to exist side by side, and because in the end they begin to appreciate such estimable qualities as each possesses. In Ontario my general impression was that their rivalry is subsiding, and that the majority is not averse to making certain concessions to the minority. Also, in the social and political ruling class as well as in business, personal relations seem to be closer. Possibly out of sheer snobbishness the French Jonahs are allowing themselves to be swallowed whole by the British whale, but it also happens that the fashionable English set is receiving distinguished members of the minority, bag and baggage, without asking any remuneration. The English play the game well, so anyone who has once been accepted is well treated.

But at bottom there is no real agreement, no fusion; in fact, a marked lack of mutual confidence exists. The French Canadians fear that their co-citizens may eventually cease to respect the guarantees of 1763 and 1774, notably in matters of education; and that if Canada indulges her instinct for assimilation she may no longer accord the French group the right to remain apart. The English Canadians, on the other hand, are suspicious of French loyalty, unjustifiably so, and above all they despise their conception of life, their papacy, their mediocre standard of living, and their birth-rate, which to an Anglo-Saxon seems ridiculous, even scandalous. Since the conquest 175 years have passed, and yet they still are not resigned to the presence of this heterogeneous element which they cannot assimilate. They tolerate it with an impatience which increases as the French

Canadians grow in numbers. The Orangemen are the noisy expression of this ill-will, but many others lend their tacit consent, and others approve almost without realizing it.

What is the real national sentiment of the French Canadians? If I can rely on what they themselves have told me, their only instinctive feeling of patriotism is towards their province, not towards Canada as a whole. French Canada, to them, is the only reality.

"The French Canadian," writes M. Louis D. Durant, "is essentially a peasant, both as an individual and in his family life. The Canadian fields, which he has often traversed, ploughed, and harrowed, are the only place he knows, and it is there that he has anchored the full devotion of his soul. The Canadian countryside is his home, his only native land." And although there came the conquest, to what extent can we say that he has been willing to share that homeland of his with the conquerors? "One day he found himself abandoned, in the presence of a stranger who did not speak his tongue, who did not worship in his way, and who, moreover, was at no pains to conceal the fact that henceforth it was he who was to be master. That day Jean Baptiste, letting his gaze wander over the horizon spread out before him, felt clearly and strongly that this was his home, and that no power, no arrogance, no astuteness could alter the fact that these houses, these fields, these churches, these roads belonged to him, and to him only." [1]

I believe that if the people in any country with a peasant population were to be questioned as to their patriotism, they would give the same reply, especially where they have experienced the vicissitudes of conquest. Therefore it is not surprising that the majority of French Canadians do not feel any real patriotic sentiment towards the Confederation. The Federal political leaders, who play their part in the government of the Dominion, have risen above this level, but even their patriotism comes from the brain rather than from the heart. When they are travelling abroad, or living in foreign countries, their homesickness may be for the Dominion as a whole, but the average French Canadian of the province of Quebec, especially the peasant, looks upon Canada merely as a cold, legal entity, to which he need not always be strictly loyal. We must remember that the man from Quebec feels as much of a foreigner in Toronto as he does in New York!

If we try to find out what they really have at heart, we shall conclude that all French Canadians desire one thing, and one thing only, and that is the development of their race as a distinct unit, and the preservation of their integrity. There are slight variations in the way

---

[1] *Les Canadiens Français et l'Esprit National* (Inquiry made by the Action Française).

this subject is approached. The clergy, especially those at the top, concentrate on keeping the French Canadians within the fold of Catholicism, which means that they must remain French within the British regime. Political leaders, like Laurier who was the most illustrious of them all, also wish to develop the French Canadian race, but they consider that the best way is for it to take its legitimate place in the Dominion. They believe in accepting the obligations arising therefrom and they favour the spread of Canadian nationalism. Bishops and Federal ministers—at any rate when they are in power —can easily agree on a joint programme of this kind.

Although it has the same general characteristics, the Nationalist conception, which really expresses the deep-seated feelings of the French Canadian people, represents a rather different point of view. No doubt it aims at the defence, pure and simple, of their own language, personality, culture, and definite political individuality, as do the others. But this sometimes differs slightly from the purely Catholic point of view, by arguing that the French Canadian should remain Catholic because it makes him a better Frenchman! There is a slight difference in meaning here, and actually many Nationalists —"dyed-in-the-wool Canadians," as the saying goes— consider that the centre of gravity of French Canadian unity is not necessarily religion. Among the young one may find traces of anti-clericalism. To those who are uncompromisingly French, the province constitutes the real environment in which they can develop a useful national activity. The Federal and the Imperial bond are mere formalities in their eyes, worthy of no patriotic sentiment, no sacrifice, and no concession whatever.

Such certainly is the outlook of the great majority of the French—at any rate this is the impression one receives the moment one sets foot on Canadian soil. This conception had already taken shape at the time of my first visit to Canada at the end of the nineteenth century. It had been brought into being partly by the persecution of the French schools in Manitoba and partly by Canada's participation in the South African War, which aroused undisguised opposition among the French. Similar circumstances, notably the Great War, have since revived the movement from time to time, never failing to rally an important section of the younger men.

§ 6

Being in possession of these various factors, we can now ascertain the political attitude of the French Canadians.

First let us consider their attitude towards Canada itself. We have already seen that the only thing that really interests them is to be free to develop in their own way. The Confederation, as it was conceived in 1867, seems very vague and distant to them, something which concerns a few of their leaders but leaves the masses indifferent. They accept it, however, but only on condition that it is strictly interpreted and that the province remains more important than the Federal organization. The men who inspired this great political act undoubtedly were desirous of unity, but since they set up provinces endowed with extensive powers, and since the Federal authority has not made a habit of imposing its superior will, local nationalisms have been allowed to continue undisturbed.

"There never has been any question of uniting the country either morally or nationally," writes M. Albert Levesque, a French Nationalist, "but simply to create a basis of political union between two conflicting nationalities, which are destined to live side by side in the same physical surroundings, where mutual assistance is indispensable. . . . To have united the two Canadian peoples in a single political state is the only moral significance of the Confederation of 1867." [1]

This interpretation shows that the Province of Quebec is afraid of a confederation which might become too powerful. In Nationalist circles the English character of the Federal administration is sharply criticized as they consider that the French element is not represented as fully as it is entitled to be. At Ottawa the atmosphere

[1] Albert Levesque, *La Jeunesse Française et la Confédération Canadienne* (Inquiry made by the Action Française).

is British, they say, and French Canadian M.P.s imperceptibly become just Canadians, which implies a compromise, and, to the Nationalist mind, virtually a betrayal.

"Our uneasiness increases," writes M. Levesque, "when a Beatty, a Thornton, a King, a Lapointe, and even a Bourassa, talk of national unity, of the Canadian nation, of patriotism which is exclusively Canadian, and all this while they invoke the spirit and the letter of the Dominion constitution."

The controversy is extremely interesting, for it involves the very guarantees of the minority's existence. Traditionally, the French Canadians have found adequate security only in the word of a foreign power, for, as they say to themselves, a minority representation in a confederation cannot possibly give the same assurances. For this reason the people of Quebec, although they have no sentiment whatever with regard to England, insist upon retaining the appeal to the Privy Council (in civil matters), and refuse to have the right to amend the British North America Act transferred from the Imperial Parliament to Canada itself. Many French Canadian leaders, who are imbued with the Federal spirit and Canadian sentiment, think differently. M. Lapointe, for example, a legal authority of first rank and a genuine French Canadian, considers that the political maturity of the Dominion has reached a point where it should be allowed to divest itself of the last traces of colonial independence, but that this should not imperil the future of the French Canadian. This is also the view of Senator Dandurand, the veteran Canadian statesman.

The logical development of Canada favours this view, which no doubt in the end will carry the day. But the underlying instinct of the French Canadian is inclined to move in another direction. We can discern a latent feeling of separatism, not as regards England, since complete independence appears to be impossible, but from the Confederation. Just as some of the English in British Columbia would willingly revert to the colonial status without Canadian allegiance, so one meets French Canadians in Quebec who say that they would like to see a French-speaking Dominion on the banks of the St. Lawrence, under the protection not of the Confederation, but of Great Britain. Perhaps this is simply the survival of a state of mind which I remember having encountered in 1898, but one cannot ignore it nor yet pass it over in silence.

If such is the sentimental attitude of the French Canadians, we may wonder what national duties they are ready to fulfil. To defend the British regime in Canada if it is attacked, no doubt, and in this connection we recall the famous saying of Sir Etienne Paschal Tasché, that "the last cannon shot on American soil in defence of the English flag would be fired by a French Canadian."

But it is not for this flag that they will march, and it would be very difficult to persuade the defenders to go beyond the frontiers. This is almost the position of the peasant clinging to his fields. If British Columbia on the other side of the continent were threatened, would the people of Quebec not be tempted to say, "Your war . . ." as once happened, it is said, at Marseilles? All the more reason should their duty to the Empire be involved.

The leaders, if they are in power and under pressure from Great Britain, cannot always decline, just as Sir Wilfrid Laurier's Government was unable to avoid participation in the South African War. But French Canadian opinion always lags behind, feeling that its only duty is towards Canada, one might even say only towards French Canada. "The French Canadian," writes M. Durant again, "is a Canadian, nothing more. His rights stop at the boundaries of his territory, and he feels and believes that there, also, is to be found the limit of his duties." [1]

These lines in their crystalline brevity admirably sum up the attitude of the French Canadians during the Great War, and the spirit in which they interpreted

[1] Louis D. Durant, *Les Canadiens Français et l'Esprit National* (Inquiry made by the Action Française).

what might be their obligations towards either France or England. As a matter of fact, they simply did not go! Out of the 619,636 men who made up the Canadian Expeditionary Force, the French numbered only about one-tenth of the total although they account for 28 per cent of the total population of the country. The famous 22nd battalion, which covered itself with glory, is only an exception to prove the rule.

During the period when the army was recruited exclusively from volunteers, the French-speaking sections of the country gave a mediocre reply to the appeal that was made to them. Later, when conscription was established by the Military Service Act of October 13th, 1917, the Province of Quebec acted like a little Vendée, for the "good fellows" were those who refused to serve, and hid themselves in the woods. The facts are neither contested nor contestable, although precise figures are not available. Of course, many French Canadians did do their duty brilliantly. So before we condemn, let us at least try to understand.

We must first avoid interpreting too rigorously the figures giving the relative racial composition of the troops. It is true that the French Canadian proportion was very low, yet we must not overlook the fact that the English-speaking contingent included a considerable number of men who had been born in the Old Country and who should honestly be classified as English rather than Canadian. In the first contingent which arrived at the front before March 1915 the *British born* accounted for 64 per cent, and out of all the volunteers who joined before conscription they made up 49 per cent. If there had been in Canada as many French born as there were British born, the French-speaking contingent would have undoubtedly been very much more important. This consideration modifies to a certain extent the contrast between the keenness of the English Canadians and the reluctance of the French Canadians. Nevertheless, taking everything into consideration it is undoubted that the French Canadian element only provided a very mediocre proportion of the Canadian army during the war.

There are no official statistics which disclose the exact number of French Canadians in the Canadian army during the war. An approximate estimate made by Colonel William Wood places the figure at about one-tenth of the total. Therefore out of the 619,636 men (the official figure), the French Canadians would have amounted to about 62,000. Although it is impossible to confirm it by reliable statistics, this valuation is probably not far from the truth.

Certain official figures do, however, allow us to get some idea of the role filled by the French element in comparison with the English.

The first contingent of 36,267 men, which arrived

at the front before March 31st, 1915, was made up as follows:

		Per Cent
French Canadians	1,245	3.4
Other Canadian born	9,635	25.6
British born	23,211	64.0
Foreign born	2,046	7.0
	36,137	100.0

The English character of the contingent (using the word English in its strictest sense) is emphasized by the fact that there were only 4,626 Catholics, or 13 per cent, whereas there were no less than 17,187 Anglicans, without counting the Presbyterians, Methodists, Baptists, and other Protestants.

The first contingent was to a certain extent optional. However, we know the origin by provinces of the volunteers who joined the army from the outbreak of the war up to October 31st, 1917. Ontario with a population of 2,527,292 gave 191,632 men, or 7 per cent of its population, and 43 per cent of the total recruits. The Province of Quebec with 2,005,776 inhabitants gave 48,394, or 2.4 per cent of its population, and 11 per cent of the recruits. This is an interesting indication, although only approximate, for the Quebec figures included alongside the French majority many English Canadians from Montreal and the Eastern Townships. The exact number of the latter cannot be given. Of course there could also be French Canadians in the contingents from the other provinces.

Altogether 45 per cent of the volunteers were born in Canada, 49 per cent in Great Britain, and 6 per cent elsewhere.

If now we study the figures for the whole Canadian Expeditionary Forces, which amounted to 619,636 men, we find that the Province of Quebec furnished 88,052 men, or 4.3 per cent of its population, and 14.2 per cent of the total army; whereas the Province of Ontario furnished 242,655, or 9.6 per cent of its population, and 39 per cent of the army. In the total figure of 619,636 there were 141,611 Catholics, or 22.8 per cent, and this naturally included many who were not French Canadians. On the other hand the Anglicans alone without the other Protestant denominations amounted to no less than 191,507, or 30 per cent of the total. This significant fact again emphasizes the English nature of the recruitment.

It appears that we may reasonably conclude from these facts that the French Canadian contingent cannot have exceeded 10 to 15 per cent of the total, although the French Canadians amounted to 28 per cent of the country's population. We have the right to say without exaggeration that the French contribution was poor in comparison with that of the English, even though the contrast is modified by the fact that a heavy proportion of the English-speaking contingent was made up of Canadians born in England, and who therefore reacted more as Englishmen than as Canadians.

Let us look into the reasons that can explain or justify such an abstention.

In 1914 French Canadian opinion ran high against the English in Ontario, who were threatening to close the schools of the minority. M. Bourassa, the Nationalist leader, had long been encouraging his compatriots to be on their guard against British imperialism. "We are ready to defend Canadian territory," he declared, "but European quarrels are none of our business!" The French Canadian clergy were all the more inclined to share this way of thinking as they had been deeply moved by the "Combist" policy, and were losing no opportunity of presenting France as a decadent country, justly meriting the wrath of God. When the volunteer army was being recruited, the French Canadians, therefore, were scarcely prepared for the surge of feeling which attracted masses of English Canadians to the colours. At the very beginning, however, before they had recovered from the first shock, the French Canadians seem to have been stirred, and they might have volunteered in greater numbers if on the one hand their parliamentary and religious leaders had urged them to do so, and if on the other hand—I wish to emphasize this—the Canadian Government had not stumbled from one blunder to another.

At that time the Canadian army was being organized by British Canadians, in the British spirit, and as a unified force, in which the desire to give the French element its proper place never seems to have existed. The recruiting agents sent into the Province of Quebec were English and Protestant, so it is not astonishing that they did not succeed! Then the minority asked for regiments of their own under French commanders. When a peasant from Quebec is lined up in a battalion in which his language is not spoken, he finds himself isolated, and a stranger, and as he was sometimes treated as an inferior, one can guess that he felt that he was being snubbed. When he joined the colours, the idea in his own mind was to serve France, and then they turned him into an English soldier! The simplest possible reaction was for him to protest that he did not want to fight for the English!

It was about the time these difficulties began to loom up that M. Bourassa intensified the Nationalist campaign, which he had been conducting for years in *Le Devoir*, with incomparable vigour. He turned down any suggestion of taking part in the war, and his influence over the Province of Quebec, and notably over the parish priests, was so great at that time that no one in French Canada dared oppose him. The Liberal opposition, led by Sir Wilfrid Laurier and recruited chiefly from the French districts, could have started a movement in favour of joining up voluntarily, had it appealed either to their loyalty to England, or to their sympathy for France, their old motherland. But the Liberal leaders were mainly busy with preventing M. Bourassa from laying hold of the entire Province of Quebec, so they halted half-way, murmuring no doubt all the right and proper things, but not giving the impression of throwing themselves body and soul into the struggle. Certainly they recognized that they had a political duty to discharge to England and a moral one to France, but they felt these duties were limited, so they talked of sending money and clothing when what was needed was men. In the end they refused to vote for conscription, and voluntarily remained outside the National Government which they had been asked to join. Behind them the local politicians did not hesitate to proclaim that French Canadians should not be sent to Europe to be killed, that they were needed in America where their work lay, and where they could safeguard the future of their race. Unless we are greatly mistaken, this argument carried weight, for it responded to an instinctive conviction that the duty of the French Canadian is to Canada—to French Canada.

It is difficult for the French to understand how such matters as the schools in Ontario or the English recruit-

ing sergeants could have been put into the balance
alongside the very existence of France, which then certainly was at stake. It was the instinct for local survival,
blind but powerful, which determined the stay-at-home
attitude. The English Canadians looked on with bitterness mingled with contempt, and when they recall it
even today their anger rises to the gorge.

"In the South African War," wrote an English
Canadian friend to me, "the French Canadians were
hostile to our taking part, from which we concluded
that they were not ready to fight for England. In the
last war their record frankly was bad, so that this time
we came to the conclusion that they could not make up
their minds to fight for France either. We are now won-
dering for whom, or for what, they would be disposed
to fight."

In truth, the foundation on which the Dominion rests
is so narrow that we are tempted to ask the disturbing
question: "Is Canada a Nation?"

§ 7

Let us now leave the solid ground of analysis, and
risk ourselves in the uncertain world of supposition.
An independent French Canada is a visionary idea—a
separate French Dominion is all that is conceivable. If
the day were to come when the French were in the
majority in the Confederation—an hypothesis which

is improbable but nevertheless not impossible—I believe that the English Canadians would not remain in the Union. If, on the contrary, the French Canadians were simply a growing minority, as is quite likely, its influence would probably be exerted in three directions: first, in resistance to Federal centralization; secondly, in persistent opposition to imperialism; and finally in a cold but reliable loyalty to the British connection for fear of the United States. We should like to remark in passing that, so long as this minority does not become a majority, the future of the British in North America can easily be adjusted to the changing situation.

If the French Canadians are to profit by their opportunity, they must show that they are capable of creating a culture of their own, for mere numbers, even if they become impressive, will not give them any real power. This culture, of which one can already discern the eventual form, will be traditionally French and Catholic, geographically American, and based on English institutions. It is doubly handicapped by being excessively dependent upon the Church, and by a provincialism which is sometimes suspicious of any close intimacy with France.

As we have already said, French culture owes a great deal to the Catholic clergy, and we do not overlook its advantages. But a regime based on such strict control is suitable for only quite undeveloped masses.

The only outstanding personalities that it promotes are ecclesiastics, as otherwise, if a man is to make his mark, he must break away completely. As the community is at present constituted, it is impossible for French culture to develop independent of Catholic culture, so the latter has necessarily a sterilizing effect. Looking back over the past fify years, we find that French Canada has produced a great number of distinguished, often brilliant, individuals, but it has not provided that collective *élite* which is essential to place it in the first rank in business, in science, in the arts, and in intellectual creativeness. What they need is prestige in their relations with the English.

There is a latent provincialism on the banks of the St. Lawrence which considers that French Canadian culture can flourish alone, on its American territory. There is also a certain distrust, from which the clergy are not exempt, which appears whenever one alludes to thoughts or ideas from France. It is a sort of instinctive retreat which is most disconcerting. When a French Canadian student returns home from the Sorbonne, he is often put under observation as if he were bringing back some contagious disease. Yet there are in France living springs of intellectual inspiration from which the young country should not deprive itself. It would therefore be worth her while if French Canada were to work for the preservation of France.

CHAPTER XIV

CANADA AND THE UNITED STATES

§ 1

THE relationship between Canada and the United States is exceptional; in fact, there is nothing quite like it anywhere else in the world.

In the first place Canada does not love the United States. On the contrary she fears her, because Canada is determined to develop her own political entity. This feeling, latent but very real, is shared by all Canadians. It is apparent among the thinking English Canadians, and still more so among the French. At the same time, and without being contradictory in any way, the Canadians undoubtedly like the Americans. An American is one of themselves, and less of a stranger than an Englishman.

Actually these two peoples have grown up like brother and sister, developing from the same colonial stock, having lived side by side, as we are too apt to forget, for 150 years before the Americans seceded. From the past they have both inherited the same faith in democratic self-government, as well as the same common patrimony of American civilization, to defend which they would soon unite. The consequence is a natural intimacy, which is as complete as that of the Siamese twins with a common circulation of blood.

The paradox of the Dominion is that in spite of being perfectly loyal to the Empire it is essentially North American. This is no mere geographical expression, for the visible signs and repercussions of this North American unity are endless. There is the same material structure in both Canada and the United States, their customs are the same in every way, the same methods of work in factories and offices, and the same amusements. Canadians like the American cinema, the American radio, American sports, and American papers, and could not do without them. An inquiry held in Kingston, Ontario, showed that of the eighty-four different journals and magazines sold in the town, only fifteen were English or Canadian. In spite of the English or Scottish influences on which we have already dwelt, the churches and universities are evolving in this sea of Americanism. But the most important feature is the standard of living which is common to both countries at the American level in contrast to the European or Asiatic level. Anglo-Saxon America is thus all in the same social level which creates an irresistible bond between the two countries. Because of the common material level of existence, the Canadians are riveted, economically and socially, to the

United States. They would never be willing to link up with Europe at a lower level, and there you have an argument against which neither sentiment nor politics will prevail.

§ 2

All the vexations in the world are not enough to enable politics to set up an effective barrier between the two countries. In daily life each of the Canadian provinces carries on closer relations with its neighbouring state across the border than it does with either England or even with the other Canadian provinces. There is a natural affiliation that is quite independent of the flag; the Maritime Provinces with New England, Western Ontario with Michigan, and British Columbia with the American Northwest. When I was in Vancouver, for example, there was a convention of combined Kiwanis clubs from British Columbia, and the states of Washington, Oregon, and Idaho. The atmosphere, which was of the utmost cordiality, was neither Canadian nor American, but—how shall I express it?— rather North Pacific. One had the impression that these groups did not include California nor the Prairie Provinces, but were the spontaneous representatives of a regional community which took no account of frontiers. This is another example of our theory of the compass and of the imperious attraction which is exerted from

North to South. It turns all the structural lines of the continent around to the vertical position.

We must accept the fact that American intimacy is inseparable from the Canadian personality. The attitude of the people towards the King and the President is particularly striking. Their loyalty to the Crown is very great, and the people sing "God Save the King" with conviction! But they talk much more about the Man at the White House, and not as foreigners either. They follow what is happening in the United States much more closely than what is happening in England. The Grangers, the Non-Partisan League, the New Era, the New Deal, and all the rest, are like domestic politics, and their repercussions have a direct and immediate bearing on Canada.

Two travellers whom I met on the road in 1935 were talking about the New Deal, President Roosevelt, and the Lindbergh case, but they were not preoccupying themselves in the slightest with England, which seemed as far away to them as China. I wondered if they even knew the name of the British Prime Minister! When it comes to telling the time, it is noon in Montreal when it is noon in New York, but it is five o'clock in the afternoon in London and nothing can be done about that!

It is the same way with trade, which, as we have seen, is like internal commerce, and is so intimate that it tends to become more competitive than complementary. Even in spite of the tariff, and other forms of official discouragement, trade adapts itself naturally to the circumstances, like vegetation, taking advantage of every opportunity and becomes absolutely irresistible.

If there exists anywhere in the world two nations more desirious of trading freely with each other, it would be difficult to find them. "Take down the fence, or even lower it by a rail or two," writes Mr. Dafoe, "and the tide of commerce rises like a flood." [1] One can easily imagine what would happen if free trade, in the Cobden sense, were effectively introduced. Would Canada be able to survive? This, from the Canadian point of view, is the explanation of their anxiety to have a tariff which will indirectly guarantee their political independence.

The barrier between the two countries is very frail. When one travels towards the West across the "great open spaces" one is no longer aware of its existence. One falls into a dollar complex—from which it is impossible to shake oneself free. Everything is American—the way one talks business, the money one spends, and even the reasons for spending it. One of my travelling companions in the train from Winnipeg to Regina explained for my benefit how Canada was being swallowed up, remarking that there is not the slightest use making any effort against it.

[1] John W. Dafoe, *Canada: An American Nation*, p. 114.

"We can't help it," he said, "it is overwhelming. The British speak of pounds, shillings and pence. What is a shilling? What is a pound? I don't know. Too far away. But I do know what a dollar is, and a cent. At the time of the Ottawa Conference an American said to me, 'The English can do what they like for aught I care. I shall go on selling to Canada just the same.' "

Do not imagine that the Canadians take these inroads of Americanization at all tragically. They submit as a matter of course, and get so little worked up that by common consent all quarrels are adjusted by commonplace discussions of what will be to the best interests of both. Even the gunshots fired across the border in pursuit of rum runners did not let loose the outbursts of passion from which Europe could so easily have stirred up a few wars. "Peace with friction for a century," as Mr. Dafoe has so justly summed up the situation.

§ 3

The Americans really like the Canadians, whom they look upon as "good fellows, and the same as our own people!" They enjoy being in Canada, for they always feel at home, whether they are living there or only visiting the country as tourists. It is calculated that, taking the good years with the bad, an average of twenty-five million people annually cross the frontier. In the holidays, or when a convention is being held (yesterday the great attraction was that Canada had escaped prohibition), the hotels are filled with animated crowds of friendly people, who roll up in droves. In the hotel lounges French embroideries and Indian birch-bark souvenirs are displayed, so that the visitors may feel that they are away on a trip, but they could just as well believe that they were still in their own home town. When they migrate to Canada for good, they are easily assimilated and soon become excellent citizens.

Ought we to believe that these good comrades, who wear their heart on their sleeve, are thinking of annexing Canada? That they once wanted to do so is evident, first in the War of 1812, and then after 1840, when Canada became autonomous and was slipping away from England; again after the American Civil War when the United States acquired Alaska; and even as recently as 1911, when the Speaker of the House of Representatives in Washington, Mr. Champ Clark, in the debate on the proposed reciprocity treaty, brought up the question of annexation in a speech which was devoid of the usual oratory precautions. Today, however, all this seems to be forgotten. The political relationship between the two countries is so rigidly correct that it could well serve as an example for others. No ulterior motive is ever allowed to penetrate these official discussions. The American interests which control Canadian enterprises are strictly careful to mind their own business.

There is no longer an annexation problem, and yet when one talks to a great many Americans, as it is so easy to do, one gathers that they consider that annexation, or some form of absorption, is inevitable.

What do the Canadians think of this prospect? As we know there have been traces of annexationist sentiment at times, and the last intrigues were still perceptible at the end of the nineteenth century. In my youth I myself was acquainted with Goldwin Smith, who was notoriously a partisan of union with the United States. But the whole British tradition militates in another direction, and counsels holding aloof. The United Empire Loyalists would turn in their graves if 150 years later Canada were to go over to the Star Spangled Banner. The Confederation of 1867 was the reply to this external temptation, and since then there have been other factors which are proving to be the true cause of Canadian unity: the completion of the Canadian Pacific Railway, then the Grand Trunk Pacific now merged into the Canadian National Railway, Canada's participation in the Great War and her glorious record at Vimy, and finally her membership in the League of Nations with a vote of her own. We may consider that this definitely settles the question.

Or, on the other hand, if we so choose, we may argue in the opposite direction. Let us consider that the discussion is still open, and examine the various factors as if they were spread out on a slab before us. The Canadians are American in custom and culture, to such a point that certain English people, especially clergymen on missions, cannot be persuaded that they can possibly be loyal British subjects. Nevertheless, they are. But when a visitor who has just arrived from the mother country takes the liberty of running down the United States, his raillery, although he is one of the family, sounds so tactless that the Canadians protest and stiffen up in defence of their own continent. Such incidents, which are of daily occurrence, suggest the following problem which will become fundamentally important in the future: With an American culture, whose centre of gravity lies outside Canada's frontiers, is it possible to found a lasting Canadian nation?

§ 4

Seen from the above angle, Canada has gained the day on two points. With regard to England, she has won her independence without breaking the connection, a satisfactory solution in every way. With regard to the United States, she has been able to make them respect her desire and her right to live her own life, and again the solution seems to be satisfactory since there is no further talk of annexation. Here we have a state with its own institutions and its own policy, but is it a nation?

Canada exists in the form of a Confederation. This

is a cold legal theory, which is accepted by the Canadians as a fact; but it does not stir their emotions. Yet when they sing "O Canada" at the end of a banquet, one can easily see that it comes from the heart. The idea of Canadian unity still entails certain reservations, especially with the French Nationalists. Similarly, whenever the logic of independence is carried a little too far, the Imperialists protest in the name of a British patriotism which goes even deeper. Are these latter really Canadians, or simply English people living in Canada?

The fact that Canada as a nation does not come first in the hearts of all her people makes one reflect. For some it is England that comes first, and for others their province; it may be that if the existence of the Canadian white race were threatened, the feeling for North American solidarity would rank above all else. The permutations of these complex allegiances can be classified like the colours of the spectrum. Thus, a Canadian can be:

1. English, Canadian, North American (a combination less frequent today than in the past).

2. French, Canadian, North American (the majority of the French Canadians).

3. Canadian, English, North American (most English-speaking Canadians).

4. Canadian, French, North American (limited to a

few of the French Canadians who have Federal interests).

5. Canadian, North American, English (a feeling which is simply latent, but which circumstances may one day bring to light).

6. Canadian, North American, French (a hypothesis included merely for symmetry!).

7. North American, Canadian, English (a common type in the past, which may reappear if the country should be absorbed).

It seems to me that I could put a goodly number of surnames under No. 1, and as many as I like under No. 2 and No. 3; but although I know some, I should have difficulty in finding many among my acquaintance for No. 4. As for No. 5, I know plenty of people whom I should range without hesitation under this heading, in spite of protestations in some cases. For No. 7 I should have to look for recruits in No. 3 and No. 5, and there again I feel that I should have no lack of names to suggest!

If our reasoning is accurate, we can see fairly well how Canadian national sentiment is being formed—or rather has not entirely succeeded in being formed. In so far as it does exist it has been inspired by leaders who are ahead of the masses, and who are certainly going farther than the mandate they received. Men such as

Sir John A. Macdonald, Sir Wilfrid Laurier, Sir Robert Borden, Dandurand, Lapointe, Bennett and Mackenzie King have conceived, realized, and consolidated a Canadian nation whose image is clear in their own minds. It is opposed, however, even among their own followers, by rival fidelities such as the imperialism of the British, the nationalism of the French, and the autonomous tradition of various provincial groups.

Nevertheless, the consciousness of a Canadian patriotism is increasing daily, and it keeps on growing as long as the Canadian state continues to exist. It is mainly a political patriotism, and it would have to be supported by a culture to acquire the foundation it needs. This is where Canada seems to be so unreal. In British North America—the very name is at once complex, contradictory, and insufficient—we can no doubt discern an English (or Scottish) culture, a French culture, and an American culture, each dominated by a centrifugal attraction. The young Canadian who is brought up according to British tradition and sent by his family to complete his studies in England, runs the risk of returning home with an English accent. Another young man, whose parents have sent him to a university in the United States to give him the education which the New World requires, will return with an American accent. The young French Canadian, little as he may wish it, is obliged to be bi-lingual if he is to succeed, and he may end up, like Sir Wilfrid Laurier and others who have earned a Federal reputation, by speaking English with a French accent and French with an English accent.

How can any true Canadian culture come out of this? The University of Laval, with its strictly French Canadian atmosphere, does not reflect the rest of the country in the slightest. Hart House, a most interesting effort at Toronto University, expresses a return to the British tradition. A business man in Toronto or in any of the little Ontario towns is an American, even if he happens to be of "Loyalist" descent and is devoutly and passionately British in sentiment; and his culture can hardly be distinguished from that of an American citizen.

We have already suggested the rudiments of a Canadian culture, which would be Anglo-French in its origins and its institutions, but American in its geographical atmosphere, with a touch of poetry and grandeur from the Far North. If it does not come into being, either because it is sterilized by tradition, choked by provincialism, or absorbed by Americanism, then the work of political creation which has now reached fruition may perhaps prove to be insufficient to assure the country's true independence.

CHAPTER XV

CANADA'S FOREIGN POLICY

§ 1

THE foreign policy of Canada is based on three essentials, which are relatively simple and easy to summarize. They are, first, the assertion of a distinct political status in international affairs; secondly, protection against menace from overseas powers; and thirdly, economic considerations, connected with the development of natural resources and the maintenance of the export trade. Whichever way we turn, we are sure to be confronted by one or other of these three propositions.

The attitude Canada adopts is a function of either her proximity to the U.S.A., her connection with Great Britain, or her international trade, which in turn depends upon the maintenance of peace. The combination would not be especially involved if the technical formation of Canada were not so diverse, but under the circumstances we must resign ourselves to a series of complicated explanations.[1]

[1] Cf. a remarkable article by F. R. Scott, "The Permanent Basis of Canadian Foreign Policy" (*Foreign Affairs*, July 1932).

§ 2

Being in North America, Canada has only one neighbour, the United States—but what a neighbour! The
relations which arise from this fact dominate her entire
foreign policy. The common boundary of over 3000
miles inevitably presents many serious problems, especially since the intimacy of the two countries leads to
continual intercourse. They are like two tenants living
in the same apartment house, indeed on the same story!
As we noted in the case of their commercial relations,
we are dealing here less with questions of foreign policy
than of the internal domestic policy of North America.
In fact it is scarcely a question of policy at all, since for-
tunately any matters to be settled are relegated by common consent to the domain of legal procedure. They
quarrel certainly, but always as one does in the civil
courts; and consequently, they do not fight. Such is the
enviable spirit in which that model institution, the International Boundary Commission, carries on its discussions. Any explanation which fails to take this geographical fact into account will miss the crux of the situation.

This gives a clear insight into the nature of Canadian
independence. It is quite obvious that the Dominion
cannot defend itself against the United States. In case
of war any resistance would be so completely impossible,
that no one ever dreams of it or prepares for it. The

only possible course would be passive resistance, with recourse to moral suasion. These remarks will seem futile to my Canadian readers, as they are convinced, and rightly so, that they have absolutely nothing to fear from this quarter.

"Canada and the U.S.A. have kept the peace for so long," writes Mr. Dafoe, "that the possibility of war between them no longer finds a place even in popular imagination. The thing to Canadian minds is inconceivable. The traditional European policies of defence, when propounded to Canadians as necessary for their security, seem amazing in their absurdity." [1]

The atmosphere of North America assuredly justifies this outlook, and though we cannot possibly compare it with European conditions, yet we can learn a lesson from it. We reflect, at the same time, that Canada—and well she knows it—is free only so long as relations are friendly, and so she dare not adopt any policy that would be liable to irritate her overwhelming neighbour. She could not, for instance, expropriate as Mexico did, the American capital invested in her territory, nor, let us say, cut off the electric power which she exports across the frontier. Therefore it is essential to maintain good relations between the two countries, and this is the cardinal preoccupation of every Canadian Government, no matter to which party it belongs. I should not be sur-

[1] John W. Dafoe, *Canada: An American Nation*, p. 93.

prised if it were uppermost in their minds, and came even before their anxiety not to annoy the English.

But we should be wrong in our interpretation if we believed that Canada feels that the proximity of the United States is not on the whole advantageous. On the contrary she considers it as a valuable guarantee of her security, since if ever she were menaced by a foreign power, the Monroe Doctrine obviously would protect her. One naturally thinks of Japan. Some tactless commentators have been known to suggest that the Monroe Doctrine would even protect her against England if the latter were to resort to force in this prescribed area. This point is ridiculous, and I am only quoting it in order to emphasize the strictly continental character of the problem. The protection of the Dominion—and those concerned are under no illusion about it—in no way depends upon the British fleet, but rather upon the military power, or, if you prefer, on the immense potential force of the United States. This is admitted by tacit understanding in view of the solidarity of the North American continent, from which England is excluded.

One might be tempted to think that the independence that Canada has won from the mother country might be lost again on the other flank, since from the moment when she is willing to rely on someone else for her defence, she has redescended to the status of a protectorate. It may be that the Dominion Government will not always be resigned to this attitude, but, up to the present at any rate, although they fully realize these conditions, Canadians do not seem to have been seriously worried by them. Taking into account the fraternal relations existing in North America, it is perfectly natural that both countries should feel that it is their duty to adopt a common policy, amounting almost to an alliance, in order to defend the patrimony of their common civilization. Public opinion, arising from this community of interests, is so identical that, on any international question whatever, the spontaneous reaction of both countries is, nine times out of ten, exactly the same. There is no need of diplomatic influence, of an exchange of notes, or of conversations between ambassadors. No, the American atmosphere, being the same on both sides of the boundary, naturally suggests the same replies, arising from the same moral reflexes from the same instinct to distrust Europe, and the same "White American" complex. At Geneva, for example, the Canadian delegate expresses a point of view which would be that of the American delegate if there were one. Close your eyes, and you might easily think that the voice of America were speaking. It is sometimes said that Canada interprets the United States to Europe, and this is perfectly true. Even when interest or prudence dictates this attitude, however, the Dominion adopts it without pressure and of her own free will.

§ 3

The British connection involves a series of relationships of an entirely different order, which maintain Canada within a non-American system, and oppose an east-west attraction to the trend from north to south. Even though she has become independent, the Dominion cannot do without the mother country. It is a question of sentiment, whereas there is none in the case of the relationship with the United States in spite of the cordiality. It is also a matter of policy, for even though the Empire may not directly provide military security, it confers a prestige which is a form of international security. Then again, England is Canada's best customer, and finally she counterbalances the American colossus, whose physical pressure would otherwise become unbearable. In the political domain this bond with the old country is just as important as is the link with the United States in the continental domain. The combination of these two elements is essential to the political existence of Canada, for her independence is made up of the equilibrium which results from this double dependence.

It is not in Canada's interest to upset this equilibrium, but rather that a tacit understanding should maintain it more or less indefinitely. If the first principle of Canadian policy is to keep on friendly terms with the United States, there is another which is not one whit less important, and that is to do everything possible to preserve cordial relations between the United States and England. Any rupture, even a serious difference of opinion between London and Washington, would put the Ottawa Government in an impossible situation, for it would not know which side to choose. Certain overwhelming arguments—geography, security, and community of outlook—might incline her to the side of the United States, but automatically there would be a passionate reaction on the part of the British element. If the point of issue were serious, this might lead to civil war and break up the entire country.

Canada is thus apt to intervene in imperial policy, and even more closely in English policy, in order to obtain solutions which are acceptable to the United States. Thanks to the good offices of the Dominion, the American viewpoint is thus represented and supported in the very heart of the Empire, which is therefore drifting towards America and away from Europe. There is nothing either astonishing or disconcerting in this when we recall that Canada herself is American.

In this connection it is curious to watch the English attitude. The British Government might be tempted to make use of Canada in order to influence the policy of the United States in favour of Great Britain. Undoubtedly various subtle influences are working in this way, but on the surface England's chief aim in this connection seems to be to avoid, at all costs, ever placing Canada in the delicate position of having to choose between either the United States or England. Now this can be prevented by adapting Imperial policy as far as possible to American preferences. It is in this spirit that time and again London gives way to Washington, and if, on behalf of the collective interests of Europe, a third party were to encourage the British Government to resist, the latter would indignantly protest, as in Corneille's *Nicomède:* "Ah, don't embroil me with the Republic!"

Such anxiety to avoid the slightest shock to a state of affairs which, though precarious, may yet be enduring, is an essential basis of Imperial policy. It must be admitted that it coincides with the desire, not only of Canada, the country chiefly interested, but also of the other Dominions. This was the attitude that General Smuts expressed with considerable force in his great speech at the banquet given by the Royal Institute of International Affairs in London in 1934.

"The Dominions," he said, "have even stronger affiliations towards the United States than Great Britain has. There is a community of outlook, of interests, and perhaps of ultimate destiny between the Dominions and the U.S.A. which in essence is only the first and the most important of them. Through the Dominions, British policy is ultimately tied up with the United States in a more profound sense, which goes much deeper than occasional jars which, perhaps, are more acutely felt at any particular moment. That fundamental affinity, coming from the past, stretching to the future, is, or must be, the real foundation of all British foreign policy. Any policy which ignores it, or runs counter to it, is calculated to have a disruptive effect on the Commonwealth as a whole. We are here on bedrock, which we ignore at our peril!"

It may be that this conception sacrifices the substance for the shadow, the shadow here being the prestige which England obtains by keeping Canada within the Empire, and this is no small thing. The role of Great Britain in international affairs would be very different, if the fear of losing Canada in a dispute with the United States were relegated to second place. The fact that it has been given first place since the war has allowed the Canadian Government on several occasions to wield a decisive influence in the determination of Imperial policy. At certain moments decisions have been taken, less in London and from the English point of view, than in Canada and from the American point of view, so that the centre of gravity of the Empire seemed actually to have been displaced. "Rome is no longer in Rome. . . ."

The most striking example was, without doubt, the termination of the Anglo-Japanese alliance in 1921. The Foreign Office, supported by Australia and New Zealand, and also by British Columbia, were in favour of renewing it, but American opinion was violently opposed. To the Americans it seemed like treason, for it broke the solidarity of the white races. Mr. Meighan, the Canadian Prime Minister, was doubtless in a better position than anyone to understand the English arguments, being British, a conservative, and an Imperialist. Nevertheless, he reacted as a North American, as he was anxious above all to avoid a policy which would not have the collaboration of the United States in the Pacific. When the Imperial Conference was debating this grave decision, he opposed renewal. His innate fear was that the Dominion might be implicated in a conflict in the Pacific, in which England and the United States would not be on the same side. Therefore it was necessary for the two great Anglo-Saxon countries to act in unison on an agreed policy, and the Conference finally rallied to this point of view. From this emerged the Washington Naval Treaty, but Canada had been able to make her own decision, and impose it on the others.

"It is not surprising," writes Mr. J. Bartlet Brebner of Columbia University, "that Canadian interest and policy revealed themselves to be quite similar to the interest and policy of the United States, for they sprang from a North Americanism whose roots in time and experience were of equal depth in the two nations." [1]

The attention paid to British policy is understandable in view of Canada's position in case of war. The Empire then is one, for when England is at war the Dominion is also. No doubt she could participate with more or less conviction, or might even do practically nothing at all, but a declaration of neutrality would be tantamount to severing her connection with the Empire. No matter how little she collaborates, however, and even if in practice she were to abstain, yet all the various alternatives imply dangerous risks either internally or abroad. A state of neutrality is feasible, but the British element in Canada would consider it treason; a passive belligerence would antagonize England, without necessarily warding off the enemy's guns; active participation as in 1914 would arouse the protests of those Canadians who do not wish to fight for what they would regard as no concern of theirs. The consequence is that Canada cannot afford to disinterest herself from any policy, even a general policy, which Great Britain might adopt, since she is dragged into a British war whether she wishes it or not. The British connection thus implies as many dangers as advantages.

It should be possible to analyse the principles which

[1] J. Bartlet Brebner, "Canada, the Anglo-Japanese Alliance and the Washington Conference" (*Political Science Quarterly*, March 1935).

determine the Canadian attitude. If England is in mortal peril, a Canadian army will intervene to help defend her, as she did during the Great War. There is no formal engagement, however, for the Canadian parliament is still master of the situation, and will make its own decision. Yet it would be impossible to refuse, for the pressure of the British element in the Dominion would be irresistible, and in an explosion of passion would carry all before it. Let us add that in such circumstances the United States would also intervene sooner or later for the same reason, to save the Anglo-Saxon civilization from disappearing from the face of the world. Thus the unity of the North American position would reappear in an unexpected form, in spite of all the palaver about neutrality.

If on the other hand it is simply a question of an "English" war, of no vital interest to the Empire, the attitude changes completely, and the Canadian Government reserves the right to act in conformity with the interests of the Dominion. No doubt there would be a difference of opinion, according to the racial origin of the population and the stage it had reached. The English would say, "Ready, aye, ready!" but the French would exclaim that the country was being dragged into an English affair which was of no interest to them. The Canadians in general, as well as their Government whether Conservative or Liberal, would consider that so long as it was not a matter of life and death they were ready to respect English interests, but that there were also Canadian interests which were equally deserving of attention. So they would lag behind, as in the Chanak incident, which was so typical, and incidentally established a precedent.

The Dominion Government confirms its right, as a matter of principle, to adopt a policy of "Canada First." It realizes that, as it belongs to the Empire, it is always liable, even in spite of its precautions, to be implicated in some new adventure. So the desire for preventive measures on its part is only natural. In order to circumscribe its responsibilities, we find it specifying that it will not be implicated in certain treaties which should be considered as English and not Imperial. For example, we have the Treaty of Lausanne earmarked in this way in 1923, and Locarno in 1925. Similarly one perceives that both beneath the surface and out in the open, Canada is exerting constant pressure to prevent the British Government from compromising itself on the Continent more than it can help. Though Canada knows full well that England must worry about and do everything possible to guard her own security, yet she always seems to be suggesting "Not too much zeal when it comes to Europe! . . ."

Another thing that it is curious to find in this British Dominion is a reflection of the distrust of "perfidious

Albion," which is so ingrained in the Americans. British diplomacy enjoys great prestige, but it is also credited with a Machiavellism of which it would be prudent to beware. "Above everything," the Canadians seem to say, "do not let us be persuaded for the sake of the bright eyes of England to embark on a policy that does not concern us!" Such is, I think, the ulterior motive in the Canadian doctrine which consists of refusing to be lined up behind England, except when she acts in the name of the League of Nations. They are afraid of being used as pawns, and believe that at Geneva they will find a guarantee against imperialism, for the latter must, at the League, subordinate itself to international demands. Canadian duties are thus submerged into a more general, and therefore less compromising, solidarity.

§ 4

Being on neighbourly terms with the United States, and one of the family in England, Canada seems at first sight to be tarred with a continental provincialism on the one hand, and with an imperial provincialism on the other.

Yet economically she has international vision, for she is obliged to export a large proportion of her raw materials. As the American and English markets cannot absorb all her production, she is forced to keep in close contact with world markets. As we have learned from her economic situation, Canada's future depends upon a revival throughout the world of a regime of international free trade—or at least more liberal ideas than at present—which will allow her to export to other countries besides England and the U.S.A. This is the price of her independence.

"More than any country in the world Canada is the result of political, not economic, forces," writes Dafoe, "and the economic disharmony between its geographical subdivisions is too great to be adjusted by policies of national exclusiveness. Unless we can trade with the outside world our condition must be one of stagnation, with a standard of living falling to ever lower levels, and with increasing strains upon the bonds that keep our federation together." [1]

We gather from this commentary, which we owe to one of the most vigorous political brains in the country, that the double chapter of Canada's relations with England and the United States does not exhaust the problem of her foreign relations. This gives her an international outlook, for it is her duty to preserve somewhere in the world a relic of economic liberalism, which depends in its turn upon the maintenance of peace, not only between England and the United States, but generally throughout the world. In this new series of relationships, which extend beyond the boundaries of the

---

[1] John W. Dafoe, *Canada: An American Nation*, p. 119.

British and North American systems, we must single out Japan, Latin America, and the League of Nations.

Having one boundary on the Pacific Ocean, Canada cannot ignore Japan. She is gradually finding that Japan can be a very satisfactory client if humoured a little. This feeling of cordiality is not wanting in Australia either. The existence of Japan, however, is manifest under another aspect, especially in British Columbia, where there is a large Nipponese colony. This colony may be more numerous than official statistics disclose, and if vigilance were ever relaxed it would probably grow at an alarming rate. On this western slope of the Rocky Mountains there is always a latent menace of inundation by the yellow race, and if the laws prohibiting immigration were suspended, this peril would loom up immediately in definite form. Even under present conditions this coast, it must be admitted, does not give the impression of belonging incontestably to the white race, and from this angle the Japanese question assumes a direct, physical character, which we in Europe can scarcely appreciate.

The hypothesis of war, though military invasion is out of the question, is certainly never out of mind, owing to the disquieting presence of this Japanese colony. This fear, however, is not felt in the East of Canada, but everywhere from Alberta westwards one detects a shade of apprehension, and British Columbia, it is no exaggeration to say, feels the same racial insecurity as Australia does. It is a very vague disquiet—hardly serious in fact—yet one cannot but think of the lines from Shelley:

> The awful shadow of some unseen power
> Floats, though unseen, among us . . .

The Canadian Government wishes to follow its own policy with regard to Japan. In 1907 a Gentleman's Agreement dealing with immigration was directly negotiated and concluded by M. Lemieux, a member of the Laurier Cabinet; an exchange of ministers plenipotentiary has taken place; and finally, Canada has shown that she is not indifferent to the organization of some defence on the Pacific coast against an eventual aggressor. We realize, however, that in actual fact her security depends upon the United States, who would certainly not be indifferent were Japan to violate Canada's territory. This situation is tacitly accepted by the Canadian people, who are ready to leave the matter in the hands of their two great protectors. The persistence of such an attitude in the Commonwealth of British Nations reveals a state of mind which is, to all intents and purposes, still colonial. Certain Canadians believe that in case of war between the United States and Japan, Canada could remain neutral, relying on herself or on the aid of England to prevent Japan from establishing bases of attack on the islands off British Columbia. Unless some such defence were provided, the United States would necessarily be driven to undertake it herself. The most probable hypothesis is that there would be military collaboration between the two North American countries. For once the position of this happy land does not appear to be enviable. It suggests Belgium in 1914, and Salonika in 1916. Let us add, however, that if the white race were threatened, North America would unite in a common defence. And this solidarity would be strong enough to overcome all other sentiments, west of Winnipeg, at any rate.

Her relations with Latin America permit us to measure, with the precision of a delicate scale, the quantity of Americanism (in the larger sense of the term) that Canada can absorb. Although invited to become a member of the Pan-American Union, where a place apparently is waiting for her, she has not seen fit to join it, up to the present time. The North American bond leads her naturally to the intimacy with the United States which we have described, but the solidarity of the New World as a whole, real as it is, seems to her to be less certain. In the northern part of the American continent there is a common Anglo-Saxon civilization, which reinforces the geographical attraction, but, in so far as the Latin countries are concerned, the Dominion feels out of touch with them, all the more so as in her northern latitude she is even farther away from them than is England herself. Her Americanism does not go beyond North America, and when it comes to proclaiming her adherence to Pan-Americanism she draws back owing to her imperial allegiance. Not that it is incompatible in any way, but she already belongs to another system which—the objection has a certain importance—is not a republican system. Therefore she is sympathetic, and may even collaborate, but always with a subtle reserve which will not let her go too far.

Geneva occupies an important place in Canadian policy. When she obtained her admission as one of the "original members of the League of Nations, signatories of the Peace Treaty," with the right to a separate vote and the possibility of accession to the Council, recognition of her new international status was assured. This satisfied her self-respect, a point on which Canadian opinion is very touchy. Though she is simply a second-grade American power, she obviously has increased her prestige by figuring separately, although in the name of the Empire, in international discussions. In this way she benefits both from being associated with the imperial community, and also from being separate from it, which is very adroit.

The assiduity with which she plays her part is largely explained by her eagerness to impress upon others that she is present, for the direct advantages she receives at

Geneva are not apparent at first sight. She is not looking to Geneva for security, since that, as we have seen, has already been provided on her own continent, where collective action in the name of the Covenant would not dare interfere. Instead one discerns a desire to contribute to a policy which is aiming at the general peace of the world, from which a country of this type derives an indirect but certain benefit. Canada's position is analogous to that of the small European powers like the Scandinavian school, who strive for an international order based on collective security. Not that she is ready to implicate herself without reserve, for her whole attitude proves the contrary. It was at her request that Article 10 of the Covenant received an interpretation which was both toned down and reassuring to her. In this country of moral uplift and devoid of territorial ambitions, people are distinctly hostile to aggressive nations.

The Abyssinian crisis clearly showed that in so far as it is British, the Canadian public reacts to the League of Nations in exactly the same way as does corresponding opinion in England and the United States. But the French Canadian section, no doubt in a spirit of opposition, acted differently, with the result that the Government, though loyal to its obligations under the Covenant, was careful not to be over-zealous. One cannot help feeling that, although collective security represents a conviction in so far as the Canadians are concerned, it is only a conviction *de luxe*. Apart from mortal danger to England, the latent temptation to isolate herself in North America is perhaps the real tendency in Canada, and the one that goes deepest.

§ 5

The argument which we have developed throughout this book leads us to the conclusion that Canada, like Belgium and for the same reasons, remains a precarious creation, and yet it is quite possible that under present conditions she may carry on almost indefinitely. She has been in existence long enough to have acquired a political personality of her own, which she naturally does not wish to relinquish.

At this point we of the Old World are constrained to ask whether it is to our interest that Canada should survive, as a member of the British Commonwealth. In view of her position and her influence in the Empire we realize that she is inclined to draw England away from Europe, and to displace the centre of gravity of the English-speaking countries by attracting it imperceptibly towards the West. In this connection it was interesting to watch the intervention of the Canadian Prime Minister, Mr. Bennett, at the International Economic Conference in London in 1933, when he urged, in fact entreated, the British Government to vote with

President Roosevelt against the whole of the European continent combined. In so doing he was working in a sense against Europe, by upholding the conception of a world-wide extra-European Empire. We may say, and not without reason, that an England freed both from the need of considering Canada and from the dependence upon America which this consideration entails, would automatically return to the fold of the older continents. This is true, but at the same time her lustre, which now serves to enhance Europe's own prestige, would, unless we are mistaken, be diminished. So Europe as well would be sorry to see the Dominion leave the Empire and retire to an entirely American setting.

So long as she remains an integral part of the British system, Canada will continue to look towards London, in other words towards Europe. Were she to detach herself from this centre of attraction she would gravitate, without any counterpoise, about the United States. Because of the present regime in Canada, the presence of Europe continues to be felt in the New World and so constitutes a paradox in an America which has otherwise entirely freed herself from the past. The thread is thin, but it still holds. In its double aspect, French and English, it still seems worth preserving, and France would certainly be extremely sorry to see it broken.

INDEX

INDEX

316; element, 91; *entrepôt* market, 180, 187; influence, 252-263; North America Act (1867), 50, 240, 269, 285; sovereignty, 230; War Cabinet, 235

Broomhall, E. J. S., wheat statistics, 157

Burpee, Lawrence J., *An Historical Atlas of Canada*, 51

Cabinet, Imperial War, 235

Canada, an American Nation, John W. Dafoe, 120, 302, 303, 313, 325

"Canada, the Anglo-Japanese Alliance and the Washington Conference," 320, 321

Canada intervenes in Imperial policy, 317

"Canada First" policy, 323; and the United States, 298-310

Canada's international status, 225-251

Canadian: accent, 256; Confederation, 48-51; dollar, 158, 219-221; Expeditionary Force, 288, 290, 291; immigrants' remittances, 215; industries, table of, 190; investments abroad, 213; Minister Plenipotentiary at Washington, 246; National Railway, 305; North, direct air route from Europe to Asia, 33; Northern Railway, 110; Pacific Railway, 33, 51, 55, 305; Problem, 28-43; unity, 307-309; universities, 182

Canadians in U. S., 122

Canadiens Français et l'Esprit National, Les, 287

Capital: American, 57, 196-198; British, 55, 197, 200, 211, 212; foreign, 210

Capricieuse, La, 65

Cardinal Archbishop of Quebec, pastoral letter, 270-273

Catholics, Irish, 94, 95

Census, 52

Centre of Population, 54

Chamberlain, Sir Joseph, 233

Champ Clark, 304

Chanak Incident, 250, 323

Chapdelaine, Maria, 33

Cheap labour, 183

Chinook winds, 38

Churches, Protestant, 98

Civil War, American, 304

Clemenceau, 267

Climate, 38, 39

Coal, 179

Coefficient of masculinity, 58-61

Colonial: Office, 232, 235; Pact, 227; Validity Act, 239

Combist policy, 292

Commissioner-General in Paris, 246

Commodities, tropical, 201

Confederation: Canadian, 48-51; Fathers of, 33

Conference: International Economic (1933), 331; Ottawa, 199, 254, 303

Conference, Imperial: (1911), 235; (1923), 245; (1926), 238, 240, 243, 249; (1929-1930), 239; War, 236

Connection, British, 316

Conquest: American attitude to, 19; European attitude to, 19, 20

Constitution, Imperial, 235

Constitutional Act (1791), 49, 269

Contrast between Europe and America, 15

Control by Church, 82

Co-operation of French Canadian clergy, 270, 273, 276

Corneille, *Nicomède*, 318

Cottons, 186

Crash, Wall Street, 198

Crown, significance of, 241, 248, 259, 301

336

INDEX

INDEX

339

INDEX

340

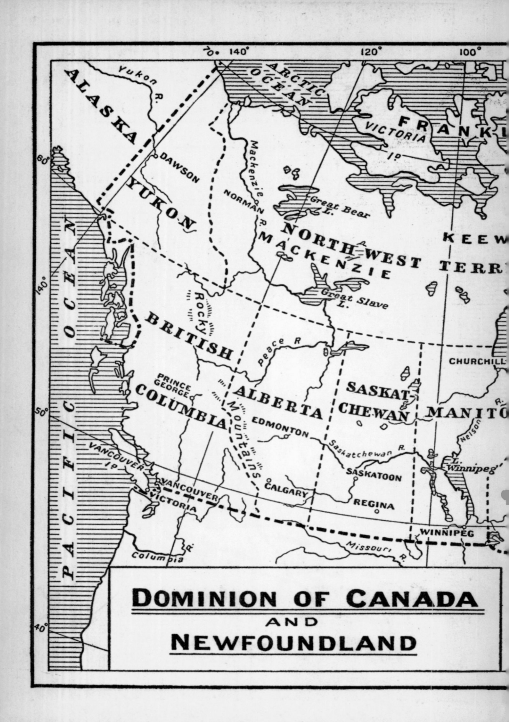

DOMINION OF CANADA
AND
NEWFOUNDLAND